A CUP OF COMFORT®

Classic Edition

Timeless stories that
warm your heart, lift your
spirit, and enrich your life

Edited by Colleen Sell

adamsmedia
Avon, Massachusetts

Published by
Adams Media, an F+W Publications Company
57 Littlefield Street, Avon, MA 02322 U.S.A.
www.adamsmedia.com and *www.cupofcomfort.com*

ISBN 10: 1-59869-534-7
ISBN 13: 978-1-59869-534-2

Portions of this volume were originally published as *A Cup of Comfort*® by Adams Media, an F+W Publications Company. Copyright © 2001 by F+W Publications, Inc. ISBN 10: 1-58062-524-X; ISBN 13: 978-1-58062-524-1.

Printed in the United States of America.

J I H G F E D C B A

Library of Congress Cataloging-in-Publication Data
A cup of comfort / edited by Colleen Sell. — Classic ed.
        p.   cm. — (A cup of comfort book)
ISBN-13: 978-1-59869-534-2 (pbk.)
ISBN-10: 1-59869-534-7 (pbk.)
1. Short stories, American. 2. United States—Social life
and customs—20th century—Fiction. I. Sell, Colleen.
PS648.S5C86 2007
813'.0108—dc22   2007017704

Contents

Acknowledgments vi

Introduction • Colleen Sell vii

The Lady in the Blue Dress • Edie Scher 1

Make a Wish, Mommy • Susan Farr Fahncke 11

The Crying Chair • Mary Marcia Lee Norwood 16

An Angel's Kiss • Susan A. Duncan 23

Finding Our Home • Jenna Glatzer. 29

Quiet Courage • Ed Nickum 35

The Well Driller • Mary Jane Chew 42

A Love That Burns Eternal • Christy Caballero 46

Of Needs and Wants • Bob Welch 52

A Special Present • Renie Szilak Burghardt 60

Drywall in the Time of Grief • Janet Oakley 66

Listen to Your Heart • Susanmarie Lamagna 73

A Daughter's Trust • David Kirkland 79

A Heaping Helping of Thanksgiving • Rusty Fischer 83

In the Arms of Grace • Lynda Kudelko Foley. 90

Maddie's Rose • Ella Magee. 96

Rejoice the Ides of March • Bluma Schwarz. 102

Not Alone • Lou Killian Zywicki 108

Gratitude Harvest • Rusty Fischer. 112

A Softer Heart • Kathryn Thompson Presley. 118

A Gift from Christmas Angels • Kimberly Ripley 126

A Stranger in the House • Denise Wahl 134

The Walk of Courage • LeAnn R. Ralph. 139

Monsters of the Sky • Louise Mathewson. 145

Memoir of a Violin • Theresa Marie Heim. 149

A Voice in the Storm • Dolores Martin. 157

Grandpa's Suitcase • Norman Prady. 162

The Colors of Prejudice • M. A. Kosak. 168

The White Dress • Helene LeBlanc 177

An Angel's Voice • Stephanie Barrow 186

The Greatest Christmas Gift • Bobbie Christmas 191

Hidden Treasure • Joy Hewitt Mann. 196

The Sweet Pea • Judi Chapman 202

Home Place • Mary Helen Straker 207

Red Two-Seater • Denise Wahl. 214

Miracle Fish • Teri Bayus. 221

The Light of Innocence • Barbara W. Campbell 227

My Dad, the Pink Lady • Lynn M. Huffstetler. 232

Holding Your Breath • Margaret A. Frey 237

Guiding Lights • Toña Morales-Calkins 246

The Blue Washcloth • Diane M. Vogel. 254

A Special Day • Anthony Merlocco 260

Sing Your Song • Lynn Ruth Miller 266

More Precious Than Gold • Denise Wahl 269

The Windfall • Audrey Yanes 273

The Saint of Subsidized Housing • Jamie Winship. 278

The Kindness of Strangers • Elaine Slater 285

I Heard the Bells of Heaven • Karen Thorstad. 291

One Night Before Christmas • Judi Chapman 300

Ah, the Dandy Lions! • Laureeann Porter 307

Tell Your Story in the Next *Cup of Comfort*® 314

Contributors. 316

About the Editor 325

Acknowledgments

I am most grateful to the fine group of people at Adams Media, especially Meredith O'Hayre, Laura Daly, and Paula Munier, who created the *Cup of Comfort®* series and brought me onboard when I desperately needed something solid to hang onto.

A heartfelt thanks goes to each of the tale spinners who contributed stories to this book.

Thanks to my husband for his love, support, and comedic relief.

Last, but most important, thank you, dear Reader, for allowing us to share these wonderful stories with you.

Introduction

"From the beginning of the human race stories have been used—by priests, by bards, by medicine men—as magic instruments of healing, of teaching, as a means of helping people come to terms with the fact that they continually have to face insoluble problems and unbearable realities."

~Joan Aiken

On the eve of Thanksgiving 1999—when I felt I had little to give thanks for—a dear friend and esteemed colleague, Paula Munier, approached me about compiling an anthology of inspiring true stories. If we do this right, Paula said, if the stories are compelling and true-to-life, if they resonate with readers and bring them a measure of comfort or hope or insight, this book

could lead to others, perhaps a series of books
. . . and you're the perfect person for the job.

I wasn't so sure, about the book or my ability to
produce it. Well into the fifth year of my son's recovery—or lack thereof—from a traumatic brain injury
and resultant neurobiological disorders, I had all but
lost my once-fervent belief in the power of story to
lift the human spirit. It was a struggle to get out of
bed and through the day, much less produce anything of value and inspiration to others.

Besides, I groused, aren't there already enough
inspiring stories out there?

No, Paula insisted. Not authentic ones. Not
compelling ones. Not nearly enough uplifting stories about the extraordinary experiences of ordinary
people. There are never too many of those.

When asked to describe Paula, the word that
immediately comes to my mind is *sunshine*. That day,
a ray of her sunshine broke through the dark clouds
obscuring my vision, renewing my belief in the power
of story and in myself. Gratefully, I took the job.

Over the next several months, as I read more
than a thousand submissions and compiled and
edited the book, something remarkable happened.
Reading about the challenges and blessings of others
helped me to face and recognize my own. It gave me,
in a word, comfort.

Then, in fall 2001, something even more remarkable happened. The book we'd spent more than a year developing, A Cup of Comfort®: Stories That Warm Your Heart, Lift Your Spirit, and Enrich Your Life, arrived in bookstores just days before and after the September 11 terrorist attacks on the United States. We could never have predicted such a tragedy, nor, in its aftermath, did we presume our book of inspiring stories would bring comfort to those reeling from that event. So we were humbled to receive numerous letters and e-mails such as these:

"The day after a national tragedy I was unsure how to deal with my grief. Your wonderful book has helped me work through my feelings, and I am ready now to talk and to listen about what happened. Thank you for understanding the need to be comforted from time to time." (Robin Coker, Sterling Heights, Michigan)

"The most memorable moment was when a young woman asked me to sign two copies—one for herself and one for a friend who had just lost her husband in the World Trade Center attack. Just knowing that our book will help give hope to those affected by the tragedy is incredible." (Susan Duncan, whose story appears in the book)

By Thanksgiving 2001, A *Cup of Comfort*® had become a national bestseller. The book's success affirmed what Paula, Adams Media, and I believed: that everyone can use a bit of comfort from time to time, and that inspiring true stories can and do give comfort.

It is not a new concept. In fact, it is as old as humanity. And these simple offerings of comfort—these real-life stories of courage and kindness, of life's blessings and miracles—are not, and should not be, reserved for catastrophes the size and scope of 9/11. We all face adversity at some point or another. We all get the blues now and then. We all sometimes get too busy, too complacent, or too mired in our problems to appreciate the positives in our lives and in others. The heartwarming stories in that first volume of A *Cup of Comfort*®—as well as in the more than twenty volumes that have followed and in the volumes still to come—remind us that we are not alone, that we can get through even our darkest days, and that there is still goodness in the world.

A *Cup of Comfort*®: *Classic Edition* includes forty-five of the fifty stories published in the first *Cup of Comfort*®—plus five new stories. I hope they warm your heart, lift your spirits, and remind you of the riches in your life.

~*Colleen Sell*

The Lady in the Blue Dress

Bridget's fingers brushed against the lump in her left breast as she showered. Her hand flew from her breast as if burned; her heart raced. Though the water was hot and the bathroom steamy, she suddenly felt chilled.

"You're a nurse," she chided herself, her voice reverberating against the tiled walls. "Pick up your hand and feel that breast again."

Bridget O'Shea closed her eyes and fearfully reached across her chest. She slowly slid her hand down from below the neck to the soft rise above her left nipple. Once again she felt the marble-like hardness beneath the skin. "Oh, please, God, no!"

Fighting panic, she hastily stepped out of the tub. "It feels like a pea," she said to the empty room. "It feels just like it says in the breast-cancer pamphlets! Oh, Mother of God, help me!"

Bridget slipped on her yellow terry-cloth robe and leaned close to the mirror, staring at her breast as she kneaded it, trying to see the lump. Water from her hair dropped down her face; when she tried to brush away the drops, she realized they were tears.

She considered calling her sister Maureen, but thought better of it. As the oldest of seven children in a household that had been dominated by an alcoholic father and with an exhausted mother, Bridget was the one her siblings always relied on. She would deal with this alone.

Bridget tried to collect herself by envisioning her mother. When she hadn't been too busy doing laundry, getting food on the table, or trying to avoid her husband's violent outbursts when he'd been drinking, her mother had been Bridget's one source of comfort growing up. She imagined her mother making a steaming "cuppa" tea, saying, "Bridget, don't waste a good worry; see how things turn out before we go ruinin' a perfectly good day." She wished her mother were there now.

Bridget shuddered, remembering the day her mother found a lump in her own breast, too late to do anything about it. The cancer had already spread and killed her in less than six months.

With trembling fingers, Bridge dialed Dr. Sheldon's number. She had been his nurse when her daughter, Molly, was in pre-school, just after she and her husband divorced. Now, twenty years later, she still used him as her gynecologist.

The receptionist wasted no time when she heard Bridget's frightened voice. "I'll push you to the top of this afternoon's appointments. Try not to imagine the worst. Some of these lumps turn out to be cysts."

Bridget knew this was true, but she also knew cancer ran in her family—not only her mother had it, but two aunts as well. Aunt Theresa had succumbed to cervical cancer following a hysterectomy at age forty, and Aunt Alice had died of lung cancer after twenty-six years of smoking two and a half packs of filterless cigarettes a day.

Preoccupied with her dark thoughts, Bridget dressed. As she brushed her thick blonde hair, another image of her mother, coaxing her to "put a little something in your belly," came to mind. When she opened the refrigerator, she gagged at the sight of the food and broke into a cold sweat.

As she sat in the waiting room of the doctor's office Bridget leafed through a magazine. The cover showed a beautiful young woman with her strong chin raised confidently with the headline "Be Prepared for Life's Surprises." Her heart sank at the irony.

The nurse made small talk to put her at ease

while Bridget slipped on a short blue patient's robe that was open in front, exposing her vulnerable breasts. She remembered sitting with her mother in this same room, waiting for the results of her mammogram. While Bridget paced, her mother sat quietly. "Bridget, don't fidget," she finally said, and they both laughed at the absurdity of the rhyme. Today, there was no one to laugh, or cry, with.

Dr. Sheldon rapped softly on the door of the examining room before walking in. "Bridget, my friend, what's this I hear about a lump?" His kind eyes peered over the top of his half-glasses.

"I felt it in the shower this morning, on my left breast."

The doctor palpated the left breast with his fingers, and then thoroughly examined both her breasts, the area beneath the collarbone, and under her arms. During the examination, Bridget turned her head away, fixing her gaze on a poster stressing the importance of a woman's nutrition during pregnancy.

When she was pregnant with Molly, her mother had made her gallons of potato leek soup. It was the only thing she could keep down the first three months. Bridget's marriage was already shaky at that time, and she had fretted to her mother about her concern over the added strain the baby would bring. Her mother had refused to let her even think of such a thing.

"This blessed baby has been given to you for a reason, Bridget. At the time, we don't always understand why things are happening, but when we look back, we know it was providence."

Mom had been right, Bridget thought. What would I ever do without my beautiful Molly? She shivered. What will Molly do without me?

"Okay, you can sit up now." Dr. Sheldon put his hand under her elbow and helped her to a sitting position.

Bridget looked directly into the doctor's face. "Did you feel it?"

"Something is there, all right. The next stop is a mammogram. But first, while you're here, I'd like to aspirate this nodule."

She knew the aspiration would tell him whether the pebble in her breast was a lump or just a cyst. The doctor performed the procedure quickly and confirmed her fears.

"The lump is firm and feels attached to the surrounding tissue, and I was unable to aspirate fluid from the nodule, so we know it's not a cyst. You know that that means it might be malignant. Then there's your mother's history to consider."

Dr. Sheldon took Bridget's hands in his and shook his head. "There is no easy way to get through this, Bridget, but it's important to move quickly. Let's schedule a mammogram for this afternoon. Dr. Brunner will read your X-rays and call me immediately. I wish I were telling you a different story."

"Tell another story, Ma," Bridget's brothers and sisters would beg their mother after dinner. They loved hearing about leprechauns in the old country. Her mother always winked at Bridget when the stories were over. "A little make-believe never hurt anyone."

Not this time, Ma. We can't afford to make believe. An hour later, Bridget had the mammogram.

Dr. Sheldon called after she returned home. "It's what we suspected. Let's get a biopsy as soon as possible."

Bridget knew that if cancerous or suspect cells were found during the biopsy, the doctor was likely to remove not only the lump but also her breast; if it had spread, he would also have to remove her lymph nodes and possibly more tissue.

"How soon?" Bridget asked. "The longer I have to wait, the more of a wreck I'll be."

"How about the day after tomorrow?" Before Bridget had a chance to complain, Dr. Sheldon continued. "It'll give you a chance to get things in order, tell Molly, take care of what you need to."

"Tell Molly? It's my job to worry about her, not the other way around," Bridget joked.

That night after a half-hearted attempt to force

down a small supper, Bridget called her daughter. When Molly answered the phone, her usually exuberant voice was a little wary. "Hey, Mom, it's Tuesday, not Sunday. What's the occasion?"

"Can't a mother speak to her daughter any day of the week?" Bridget sassed. She wanted to sound upbeat and optimistic, but there was no sense beating around the bush.

Molly reacted swiftly. "I'll be there in a few hours."

"Molly, it's too dangerous to drive a hundred miles late at night after hearing unpleasant news. Besides, don't you have to clear it with your boss to get time off?"

"Let me worry about that. I want to be with you for the biopsy. Keep the porch light on." Molly said. "Mom . . . I love you. Kisses over the phone."

Bridget let go of the tears she'd fought all day. Kisses over the phone—just like Ma used to say whenever we called her. Kisses over the phone, indeed, Bridget sniffled.

The next morning Bridget was admitted to the hospital. She was given the routine pre-operative tests and spent the rest of the day waiting. Molly, bless her soul, kept her company the whole time. An aide brought in Bridget's dinner tray. Molly picked up the lid and drew back.

"Whew! You'd have to be really sick to eat this!" Bridget laughed and pushed away the tray.

"Save the Jell-O, though, Molly. They can't do too much to ruin Jell-O. Maybe I'll feel like eating it later." Bridget reached up to pat her daughter's cheek. "In the meantime, toots, I'm feeling pretty tired. Everything is catching up with me, I guess."

Molly leaned over and hugged her tightly. "We'll get through this, Mom. Don't worry. We're a tough team." Bridget held onto her daughter and kissed her one last time before saying goodbye.

On the way out, Molly stopped to chat with Bridget's roommate, a young woman who'd had a tumor removed from her kidney the day before. "Keep an eye on my mother, would you?" Molly winked. "Don't let her try to sneak out of here without paying her bill."

Bridget and her roommate laughed and shooed Molly out of the room. Although exhausted, Bridget couldn't turn off her mind. She tossed and turned, unable to sleep.

Finally, she closed her eyes for a few seconds. When her lids fluttered open, she thought she saw her mother standing next to her bed. Funny, she was wearing the beautiful blue lace dress she'd worn to all the family weddings, the one she'd loved so much and had asked to be buried in. Bridget felt her mother's hand smooth a stray lock of hair behind her ear and whisper, "Bridget, my girl, I don't want you to go through what I did." She felt her mother's lips brush her cheek. She snuggled deeper under the thin blanket and fell into a sound sleep.

Bridget woke the next morning in the recovery room and, still groggy, reached over to feel for her left breast. It was still there. Thank God! The lump was benign. Oh, God! Was it too far gone? Had Dr. Sheldon taken one look, decided her fate, and just closed her up? Relief quickly gave way to panic. She called for the nurse.

There was a flurry of activity around her, and Dr. Sheldon strode in, a concerned look on his face.

"Bridget," he began haltingly. "I don't know what to say. . . . It's the strangest thing. . . . We went in to remove the nodule, but nothing was there. I looked at the mammogram to make sure I wasn't operating on the wrong breast, but there it was clear as day on the film."

He took a deep breath. "But there is no sign of tumor—nothing at all—in your breast tissue. It was as if we had the wrong patient on the table."

Bridget felt her breast, looking for the lump. She found nothing.

"Where did it go? Could there be some sort of mistake? Has this ever happened before?" she riddled him with questions.

Dr. Sheldon raised his hands in a helpless gesture. "I have no answers. I really don't know how to explain it. The nurses in the operating room, the interns, the anesthesiologist—all of us, we couldn't believe it. We'll do another mammogram, but for now, let's be glad for a minor miracle."

Meanwhile, Molly walked into Bridget's room holding a bouquet of daffodils. Seeing the empty bed, she turned to her mother's roommate. "Not back from surgery yet?"

"No," the young woman answered. "But don't worry. I stayed in recovery a long while, too. Sometimes they're short-staffed and can't find anyone to wheel you back right away."

"I'll wait. I want to be here when she comes back." Molly rested the flowers on the window ledge. "By the way, did my mom have any company today?" Even though her parents were divorced, Molly had called her dad and was hoping he'd stop by.

The roommate propped herself up on one elbow, thinking carefully. "No, no one stopped by today. But your mom did have a visitor last night after you left. I don't know who she was, but she was wearing the most beautiful blue lace dress."

~Edie Scher

Make a Wish, Mommy

It was my twenty-eighth birthday, and I was seriously depressed.

My whole world looked dark, my future dim. I was a newly divorced mom, raising two small children on my own. My six-year-old son, Nicholas, was in kindergarten, and I was a junior at the local university. I had taken off the quarter, because my five-month-old daughter, Maya, had been very ill.

Alone at home with two young children most of the time, I had little social interaction that winter. Even the weather seemed to be working against me. I hadn't lived in Utah long and was I still adjusting to the cold and snow. That January was one of the most brutal in years. The snow was literally thigh-high, which made leaving the house a daily struggle and added to my sense of isolation. It had been a winter of unbearable loneliness, struggle, and despair.

Feeling sorry for myself had become comfortable for me. Depression had become so second-nature I no longer remembered the happy person I used to be— or the last time I'd laughed.

The day before my birthday, I was a grouch. I felt the painful absence of the friends I'd moved away from, with whom I'd always celebrated my birthday. There'd be no party, no gifts, no birthday cake—not even a birthday phone call. I was too poor to afford a telephone.

A cloud of hopelessness hung over me as I tucked the children into bed that night. My little Nick wrapped his chubby arms around my neck and said, "Tomorrow's your birthday, Mommy! I can't wait!" His blue eyes sparkled with anticipation.

Unable to return my son's enthusiasm, I kissed his sweet rosy cheeks. I hoped he didn't expect a birthday party to magically appear, like it did on his birthday. Life is so simple when you're six.

The next morning, I awoke before the children and began to make breakfast. I heard noises in our tiny living room and, assuming Nick was up, waited for him to come in to eat. Then I heard him talking to Maya, sternly telling his baby sister to "make Mommy smile today."

His words stopped me cold, and it suddenly hit me. I'd been so wrapped up in my misery I hadn't realized how it was affecting my children. Sensing my unhappiness, my little boy was doing his best to do something about it. His thoughtfulness and my selfishness brought tears to my eyes. I knelt down in our small kitchen and asked for the strength to somehow find happiness again. I asked God to show me some beauty in my life, to help me see, to really see—to really *feel*, what blessings I had.

Putting a smile on my face, I marched into the living room to hug my children—and was again stopped in my tracks. There sat Nick on the floor, Maya on her blanket next to him, and in front of them was a pile of presents. A birthday party for three.

I looked wide-eyed and open-mouthed at the pile of presents, then back to my son. "Happy Birthday!" he cried, wearing his adorable, toothless grin. His animated face beamed with delight at the shock on my face. "I surprised you, Mommy, didn't I?"

Stunned, I knelt down next to him and asked how in the world he'd managed to get me the presents. He reminded me of our trip to the All-a-Dollar store, and I immediately recalled him telling me he was going to spend the allowance he'd been saving for ages. I had laughed at his bulging pockets and remembered thinking he walked like John Wayne, his pants loaded down with his life savings. I had almost chided him for spending everything he had so carefully saved, but thinking better of it, had done my shopping while he did his. I remembered his gleeful smile and giggles as he clutched his bag to his chest. I'd assumed he'd bought something fun for himself; I would never have imagined that the surprises tucked inside were for me.

Looking at the beautiful pile of presents in front of me, I blinked my eyes in disbelief that my darling son had emptied his crayon bank for me.

There. I heard the voice in my heart. These are your blessings. How could you ever doubt them?

My prayers had been answered. I suddenly saw the beauty in my life. The sadness lifted from my heart, and gratitude for the many blessings I'd been given filled it.

I hugged my son and daughter and told them how lucky I was to have them in my life. At Nick's eager prompting, I carefully opened each present. A bracelet. A necklace. Another bracelet. Nail polish. Another bracelet. My favorite candy bars. Another bracelet. The thoughtful gifts, each wrapped in gift bags and wrapping paper purchased with a kindergartener's allowance, were the most cherished I've ever received. The final gift was Nick's personal favorite: a wax birthday cake with the words "I love you" painted in fake frosting across the top.

"You have to have a birthday cake, Mom," my oh-so-wise little one informed me.

"It's the most beautiful cake I've ever seen," I told him, choking back tears. And it was.

Then he sang "Happy Birthday" to me in his sweet little-boy voice.

"Make a wish, Mommy," he insisted.

I gazed into my little boy's shining blue eyes and couldn't think of a single thing to wish for.

"I already got my wish," I whispered. "You."

~Susan Farr-Fahncke

The Crying Chair

While I was growing up, each chair at our family's kitchen table was spoken for. We kids had made our selections in the same sequence as our birth order—first come, first served, you might say—starting with me (the oldest) and followed by my sister, Gloria, and by my brothers, Bret and Terry. Mom didn't seem to mind where she sat.

I had picked the chair directly across from Dad. Everybody knew it as "Marcia's chair." Sometimes, however, I would give up my chair for guests and it would become known by another name: the Crying Chair. Family, friends, and neighbors would sit in that chair when they needed a good cry, or someone to share their burdens with.

We're a family of natural-born weepers, from my parents, Natalie and Jewell Bush, right on down the line to all four of their children, now grown with little weepers of our own. Not that our lives have been filled with extraordinary tragedy or that our hearts are filled with sorrow, it's just that crying is comfort for the soul.

Mom said it was only natural for "Marcia's Chair" to become the official "Crying Chair," since I was the most tenderhearted crier in the family. I put the Crying Chair to good use throughout my life. It was my crying throne when our dog Millie died; when my Dad was injured in a terrible car accident, and when he sang us a song about a little crippled girl; when I watched Superman take a crippled boy on a Super flight on our black-and-white TV; and when my two-year-old brother, Terry, tried to *be* Superman and jumped from the neighbor's tall slide. I took to the Crying Chair when my boyfriends broke up with me, and when I broke up with my boyfriends.

Yet, I was not an unhappy child. In fact, quite the opposite: I was very happy. The Crying Chair gave me a place to park my emotional baggage so I could get on with my life.

There were also times when I took to the Crying Chair with tears of joy—each time my sister, Gloria, and I were chosen for the cheerleading squads; when I was elected class officer; when I was crowned the Sweetheart Queen; when I left for college; when

I came home from college; when I became engaged, and when I became pregnant with each child.

Of course, I always graciously relinquished "Marcia's Chair" when someone else needed to sit a spell in the Crying Chair. Fran and Bob, for example, who lived across the street from us and shared coffee and stories at our kitchen table, sat there when it was time to share their tears. To this day, folks still come to sit in the Crying Chair, which still resides in my parents' home. Fran and Bob moved away from the neighborhood, but when Bob died, Fran returned to the Crying Chair.

The Crying Chair worked so well throughout the years that I decided to borrow the idea for my kindergarten classroom at a private Christian school, where I had taught for seven years. The idea came to me when I was trying to find ways to console one of my kindergarten students, who would cry uncontrollably every morning when he arrived at school and several times during the day. His parents were going through a divorce. The little guy was shifted from one parent to the next, and he never knew who would bring him to school or pick him up.

With great pomp and circumstance I announced the arrival of the Crying Chair to my classroom. It was just a regular chair that I had moved to an isolated part of our room and by which I had placed a box of tissues. The students listened with wide eyes as I proclaimed the rules for the Crying Chair. They even added a few of their own.

Rules for the Crying Chair

1. *Teacher:* The Crying Chair is *not* a punishment or time out.

   Students: We won't get in trouble.

2. *Teacher:* Raise your hand and state your need for the Crying Chair. Permission will be granted.

   Students: Ask the teacher first.

3. *Teacher:* Students who use the Crying Chair should keep their outbursts to a moderate level of noise, so as not to bother the other students or draw attention to themselves.

   Students: No screaming.

4. *Teacher:* Length of stay in the Crying Chair is up to the individual; five-minute intervals are suggested but may be extended if necessary.

   Students: Get it over with.

5. *Teacher:* The Crying Chair is available to both students and teachers.

   Students: Teachers cry, too?

6. *Teacher:* Other students will not be permitted to harass or make fun of anyone in the Crying Chair.

   Students: It's okay to cry. Don't start a fight.

7. *Teacher:* Other students are encouraged to pray for and show special kindness to the person in the Crying Chair.

   Students: Be nice. Be kind. Pray.

The students had almost a reverence for the Crying Chair. When the little boy who wept uncontrollably sat in the Crying Chair, he would bury his little head in his hands and sob. My heart ached for him, but I rejoiced as I watched other students spontaneously bow their heads in prayer for their classmate. Some asked for permission to walk over to the Crying Chair and give the boy a pat on the back—or a hug. Other times a classmate would quietly place a piece of candy for him on the table beside the Crying Chair. After a brief time in the chair, the boy would dry his eyes, ask for permission to get a drink of water, and go to the bathroom before returning to his regular seat in class. Not one student teased him about sitting in the Crying Chair. As time went on and the boy's life began to take on some semblance of order, his trips to the chair became less frequent.

The Crying Chair worked so well the two years it was in my classroom, that I wished I had thought to use it the previous five years of my teaching career. I know it would have come in handy on each last day of school, when the eyes of students and teacher inevitably welled with tears.

Many students sat in the Crying Chair for many different reasons. Sometimes it provided a safe place to cry out the everyday trials and tribulations of being a child: skinned knees and playground scrapes; embarrassment over a spilt juice container; the panicked frustration of a lost field-trip slip; hurt feelings at being called a name, or shame from being the name-caller. Sometimes the source of their tears was more traumatic, like the loss of a pet or a grandparent. For three children who had been abandoned by their mothers and were being raised by other family members it provided a soft place to fall, and to cry. One student, who strived so hard for perfection in printing that his whole body shook, found that weeping in the Crying Chair helped relax him enough to try again. One child sat and sobbed—until I thought all our hearts would break—after having been molested by a neighbor.

One particularly trying day, when I felt overwhelmed with the duties of teaching and motherhood and marriage, I announced to the class that

I needed to spend some time in the Crying Chair. I laid my head in my hands and cried. As the tears flowed down my cheeks, I felt the touch of many tiny hands as my students walked by and gently patted me on the back.

The teacher learned compassion from her students.

The students learned a teacher hurts just like they hurt, and cries just like they cry.

Both learned to love each other.

~Mary Marcia Lee Norwood

An Angel's Kiss

The first Christmas without Mom was going to be difficult. She had been the heart of the family, and her sudden death earlier that year had numbed all who loved her—especially my usually strong father, who had been reduced to a mere fragment of himself. My mother had adored Christmas and had always made it a festive and memorable holiday. While I was growing up, she had filled our home with decorative holiday splendor, the delicious aromas of holiday treats, and the merry sound of her voice singing favorite Christmas carols. She had expressed a childlike jubilance over the Christmas season that had never faded with the years. Her inherent generosity was especially apparent during the holidays.

The void left by the passing of our beautiful blonde angel, who always saw the good in every

23

human being and whose warmth had drawn people to her, would be most sorely felt at Christmas. As the holiday approached, I tried my best to emulate my mother's Christmas spirit, hoping to ease my family's sorrow by continuing her joyous tradition. I felt that I especially needed to stay strong for my children and for my devastated father. To cope with my own sadness, I kept busy. As Christmas drew nearer, however, I found it increasingly difficult to contain my grief.

My forty-minute drive to work each morning was particularly tough, as it allowed me too much time to think. I'd envision my mother baking Santa cookies or stringing popcorn for the tree or giggling at her ingenuity in finding the perfect gift for one of us and my heart would ache. Try as I did to push away these tender memories, they just crept back in. Turning on the radio was no help; the first few bars of a familiar Christmas tune would trigger a deluge of tears.

My mind flashed on scenes of happier holidays I had known as a child. I recalled the warm, cozy Christmases both in my parents' home and at my grandmother's house, when our whole family was together. My grandmother's old-fashioned, turn-of-the-century brownstone in Woodhaven, Queens, had been about an hour's drive from our house. I always thought Grandma's quaint town resembled a Dickens village during Christmas time. I remembered how the bells at St. Thomas the Apostle Church, where my grandmother was a member, chimed in succession in one key—Bong! Bong! Bong!—then, half an octave higher—Bong! Bong! Bong!

Grandma had always placed a white tabletop Christmas tree in the window of her front room. The lights on the tree were candle-shaped glass tubes, filled with different colors of liquid. When the tree was plugged in, they bubbled—much to the delight of us grandchildren. The Victrola in the living room, just off the front room, played Grandma's original 78-rpm records, like Jimmy Boyd's "I Saw Mommy Kissing Santa Claus" and Bing Crosby's "White Christmas."

Bombarded with those memories, I felt myself slipping into complete despair. "Oh, Mom. Oh, Grandma," I silently cried. "I miss you both so much. Please, I need you here with me."

Just then, an old woman standing by a stop sign on the side of the street began to frantically flag me down. I stopped my car at the sign, and to my astonishment, the woman opened my unlocked car door and sat down in the passenger seat beside me. She told me that her bus had never arrived at the bus stop and she was cold. Something about the woman seemed vaguely familiar. She asked me to take her to the local church. Though I was befuddled, I sensed no danger and agreed to give her a ride. As we drove, I asked her where she was from.

"I'm originally from Woodhaven," she replied.

That was what was familiar! She had the same warm tone of voice and unmistakable Queens accent that my grandmother had had.

When I stopped at the next red light, I turned to look at the woman's face and found myself looking right into my mother's eyes. They were the same hazel shade as my mother's and glowed softly with the same kindness. These were the eyes that had comforted me when I was upset, twinkled with joy over my happiness, and radiated love throughout my life. Shaken and confused, I pulled over to the side of the road to gather my wits.

Suddenly, I broke down. Sobbing, I told her of my grief and my haunting memories. The old woman comforted me, patting my back and cooing reassurances. The experience felt entirely surreal. After a short while, I regained my composure and apologized to the poor woman, who, I was certain, was regretting her decision to get into my car. But she seemed unperturbed by my outburst, and her calm demeanor led me to believe many others had probably cried upon her shoulder. Feeling calmer, if still shaken, I was able to drive the short distance to her destination.

We spent a few minutes parked in front of the church, talking and reminiscing about Christmases in Woodhaven. The woman knew exactly where my grandmother lived, and had also been a member of St. Thomas's Church. She also agreed that Woodhaven looked like a Dickens village during the holidays. Our conversation turned from the past to the present, and she told me about her late husband, children, and grandchildren, and about her difficulty adjusting to living in suburbia. Too soon, it seemed, it was time for us to go.

The woman placed her hand on the door handle to exit my car, then stopped and said she would pray for my family and me. Then she gently kissed me on the cheek.

As she stepped out of the car and onto the sidewalk, I realized I didn't know her name. When I called out to ask, she turned back, smiled sweetly, and said, "Dorothy."

I stared after her, dumbstruck, as she slowly walked up the church steps and disappeared through its arched doors.

Dorothy was both my mother and grandmother's names.

As I pulled away from the church and continued my drive to work, a great weight seemed to lift from my shoulders. A profound sense of comfort and peace cradled me throughout that holiday season and for all those to come. On that first Christmas without my mother, I received a message of hope and eternal love—sent by my Christmas angels through the open heart of a complete stranger.

~Susan A. Duncan

Finding Our Home

My fiancé, Anthony, and I were excited about shopping for our first home. We called every real estate agent in town, searched through newspapers and Web sites, and drove all over the city in search of "for sale" signs in neighborhoods we liked. Our funds were limited, though, and none of the houses in our price range seemed quite right for us.

One agent was especially persistent in trying to get us to look at a particular house. Although her description of the house sounded wonderful, the price was way out of our range, so we told her no thanks. She called again, suggesting we look at it before ruling it out. Again, we said no thanks, no way. But she kept calling back, urging us to at least drive by.

We finally did and it was love at first sight. It was Our Home, the one we'd fantasized about every time we talked about our "perfect house." It was small and charming and overlooked a pristine lake with tiny islands in which grew weeping willows. The property was beautifully landscaped, with a greenhouse in the backyard. We decided we just had to see the inside.

We immediately called the real estate agent and made an appointment. As we walked through the rooms, we squeezed each other's hands; we both felt the love within the walls of that home. There was a history there. Every loving detail of the tidy, cozy house reflected the warmth and character of the marriage that obviously had flourished there. Rows of plants and crafts adorned the shelves, and two fireplaces added to the romantic aura. The owners were very nice to us. Both were horticulturists, and they were amused by our awe of their incredible gardens and landscaping. The house tour became a visit, and we spent hours with them, talking about their house and our plans.

The next day, we brought our parents to see it. Just before we left, the husband told me he and his wife had moved in thirty-four years ago, right before they got married. Then he smiled and said, "Little lady, I sure hope you buy this house."

"I do too," I said, unable to hide my hopefulness.

As perfect as it was, the fact remained it was beyond our means, and we continued to look at other homes. But the little house by the lake kept calling us back. Every day, Anthony and I would drive to the other side of the lake and sit on a grassy knoll to look at the property and dream of what it would be like to live there. With our arms wrapped around one another, we'd talk about all the memories we'd create there, we'd pretend it was our house, our gardens, our lake. Once, we even took some photographs of ourselves sitting by the lake with the house in the background. Even if we could never afford such a house, we'd save those pictures for inspiration, to remind ourselves of what our dream house looked like.

Finally, we decided to make an offer—far below the asking price. We didn't expect the owners to accept it or to even seriously consider it, but we knew we couldn't live with ourselves if we'd never tried. To our surprise, they didn't laugh at us. Instead, they made a counteroffer. Of course, the counter was also much more than we could afford, but it was far less than the original asking price.

We told the real estate agent we'd think about it overnight. In the meantime, we planned and schemed about how we could possibly come up with the extra money. We asked family and friends for help, and we arranged to take on extra work. The next day, we called to make a new offer, slightly higher than our first one, still shy of the owner's counter price.

We were thrilled when the real estate agent said she thought the owners would accept it and that she'd call us back later that day with an answer. We went out to breakfast to celebrate. We were on cloud nine, tripping over our sentences as we talked about starting a People Who Live Around The Lake Club, about what kind of vegetables we'd grow, and about how we'd build a bridge to the island with our favorite weeping willow tree.

When we got back to my apartment, we were greeted by a frantic message from the agent telling us we'd been outbid—by a lot! She was calling to give us a chance to match the offer before she went back to the owners.

My head spun. This wasn't supposed to happen! How could we come so close to our dreams, only to have it pulled out from under us so quickly? I couldn't breathe. There was no way we could match the offer. My father offered to make up part of the difference between the two bids. I wanted to curl up in a corner and forget the whole thing, but Dad and Anthony weren't ready to give up.

"We'll go to the owners and talk with them directly, before the agent tells them about the new bid," Anthony said.

I was shaking head to toe, but agreed to try one last thing to live in the home we knew was meant for us. When we arrived at the house, we found the real estate agent standing in the living room, already presenting the other buyer's bid.

We decided to go through with our plan, anyway. We made our final offer, which still was thousands of dollars less than the other buyer's bid. We knew it, but we also knew we had to try.

"Sold!" The owner turned and said, "Done. Take it off the market." Our jaws dropped. He looked at us with tears in his eyes and explained.

He'd seen us all those times we'd sat by the lake. We had no idea he could see us, but he'd watched out his window. Neighbors had called, worried we were spying on the house; he assured them we were supposed to be there. He knew how much we loved the place and that we'd appreciate the years of work he and his wife had put into their home. He said he realized he was going to take a loss by selling it to us, but it was worth it. We were the people they wanted to live there. He told us to consider the difference in the price "an early wedding present."

I, too, had tears in my eyes, as I hugged him, touched that this generous couple was giving up thousands of dollars to help a young couple live their dreams.

That is how we found our home and how I learned that when people are kind, there are no strangers. Only friends we haven't yet met.

~Jenna Glatzer

Quiet Courage

My father lived a hard-working, middle-class life. He had served his country during World War II and held tight to the moral values he gained through the struggles of that era. In all the years of my youth, I knew of only two days of work that Dad missed. His honorable work ethic and quiet, solid manner also gave rise to one of his flaws, for my father was usually unable to express his feelings or to speak aloud about the love he felt for his family. Yet there was one exception to this rule that I will never forget.

One Sunday, my sister, one of my brothers, and my wife and I had gathered at my parents' house to feast upon Mom's wonderful cooking. During the normal dinner chatter, I noticed that my father slurred his words now and then when he spoke. No one mentioned this during dinner, but I felt compelled to discuss it with my mother afterward, as we sipped coffee alone together in the kitchen.

"He says his dentures don't fit anymore," Mom explained. "I've been bugging him for weeks to make an appointment with the dentist, but he keeps putting it off."

"The problem isn't his teeth, Mom. I don't know what's wrong, but he needs to see his doctor, not his dentist. I know he hates to go to the doctor, and I'll help you drag him in if we have to. I'm really worried."

Drawing on the lessons learned from her many years of marriage to a stubborn man, my mother devised a plan to deliver her husband to the doctor's office without a struggle. She made an appointment with the dentist, and then called the doctor to explain the situation. The doctor, well aware of the difficulty in getting my father to keep an appointment, went along with the plan. Waiving the normal rules for a specific appointment time, he agreed to see my father immediately after his dental appointment. The dentist, also clued into the conspiracy, pretended to adjust my father's dentures and then sent him on his way.

Mom took the "scenic route" home, and before he suspected a thing, Dad found himself in the parking lot of the medical complex. After the standard protest, he quietly followed my mother into the doctor's office.

She phoned me two days later.

"I'd like you to come over this evening. We need to talk," she said, her normally clear, strong voice breaking with the stress of bad news too painful to disguise.

I rushed over after work. Dad was lounging in his favorite chair as he watched the news and sipped a glass of beer. Smiling and appearing in good spirits, he asked how I was doing. My mother motioned me into the kitchen. She spoke softly so he could not hear. The bomb fell.

"They found a brain tumor. It's too large at this point to operate. They're going to try to shrink it with radiation and chemotherapy; maybe they can do something then." She stopped to wipe tears from her eyes. "But the odds are long."

"Dad's a fighter," I reassured her. "He's beaten a stroke, a heart attack, and lung cancer. Maybe he can beat this, too."

Even as I spoke of hope, my stomach knotted in fear. It must have shown, because my mother hugged me fiercely.

My father soon began to undergo a barrage of treatments. One of the side effects was the loss of almost all of his thick black hair. One of the lighter moments we experienced during this ordeal was when my wife, Michele, gave birth to our first child, and we all laughed to discover what had happened to Dad's hair: Chelsey arrived in the world wearing it.

My father's condition worsened, and the doctors finally informed us that his condition was terminal. During one of his prolonged stays in the hospital, we brought Chelsey with us when we visited him. By this time his speech had deteriorated to the point where interpreting the words he tried to form was virtually impossible. Lying in bed, my father's head propped up on pillows, he tried to communicate with me through grunts and hand gestures. I finally figured out that he wanted me to set Chelsey on his stomach so he could make faces at her.

With my father's hands wrapped around her tiny waist, Chelsey sat on her grandpa and they jabbered nonsense-talk back and forth. Chelsey's vocabulary was restricted by her youth, my father's by the horrible disease that was stealing a larger part of his brain with each passing day.

Dad remained in control of his laughter, if not his speech. And how he laughed that day. He mumbled and cooed to Chelsey; she returned the volley with a stream of gurgles and slobbery consonants. Then they'd both erupt into deep belly laughs. The bond that grew between grandfather and granddaughter never required a formal language. Dad discovered an ally who fell in love with him completely and unconditionally. Chelsey possessed the child's knack of knowing a grandfather's loving touch when she felt it. English was optional, bushels of love mandatory.

After Dad escaped the hospital for the familiar and comfortable surroundings of his own home, the Grandpa/Chelsey comedy routine became a regular part of our visits. Both participants found it hilarious. They laughed every time they played the game, each trying to out-silly the other, the love shining brightly in their eyes.

Watching the two of them together as both a father and a son, I realized I was living an experience that would stay with me forever, and a bittersweet blend of joy and sorrow overwhelmed me. I knew that their special relationship was destined to be far too brief. Though grateful for the times they could share, I couldn't shake the feeling of a clock ticking in the background. God granted them the wonderful gift of their mutual admiration society; cancer turned their potential years together into precious short weeks.

On a visit to my parents' home during what we all knew were my father's last days, my mother took Chelsey from my arms and announced, "Your father would like to see you alone for a minute."

I entered the bedroom where my father lay on a rented hospital bed. He appeared even weaker than the day before.

"How are you feeling, Dad?" I asked. "Mom said you wanted to see me. Can I do anything for you?"

He tried to speak, but I couldn't make out a word.

"I'm sorry, but I can't understand you," I said, a lump of cold steel forming in my throat. "You want your pad and pen?"

Ignoring both my suggestion for his pad and pen, which he detested, and the mechanical controls for raising the head of his bed, he slowly and with great effort pulled himself higher in the bed. The strain of concentration played out on his face.

Moved by the intensity of his struggle as he again tried and failed to speak, I reached out to hold his hand. Our eyes met and locked, both of us suddenly forced to face the painful reality that all the years we'd spent together, as I'd grown from a child to a man with a child of my own, had come down to this one last father-and-son moment to be wrested away from the wrath of cancer by my dad's sheer determination.

Tears glistened in my father's eyes. He shook his head and smiled at me as if to say, "Ain't this just the damnedest thing?" Then Dad took a deep breath and won one final battle with the disease that would soon win the war.

He softly spoke three little words with crystal clarity: "I love you."

We don't learn courage from heroes on the evening news. We learn true courage from watching ordinary people rise above hopeless situations, overcoming obstacles they never knew they could. I saw the courage my mother possessed when she chose to fight the battle that would allow her husband to remain at home where he belonged. I gained courage from our friends, neighbors, and relatives as they drew closer, circling wagons of love around us in the last days of my father's life. Most of all, I learned about courage from my father, who simply refused to leave this world until he overcame his greatest obstacle: sharing his heart with his son.

~*Ed Nickum*

The Well Driller

This is a story you won't find in the newspapers today. It didn't change the world, the course of events, or even someone's mind. It isn't complicated or deep. It's simply a story about a good man who did a great thing.

Leslie M. Chew was my grandfather. He drilled water wells in Indiana and started his business during the Great Depression. Although nearly everyone was out of work, people still needed water, so he didn't lack for jobs. Most of his drilling was for residential properties in the small towns amid the flat plains so well suited to farming.

Even during those tough times, Gramps never used a written contract for his business. He had faith in the integrity of his neighbors, and he always believed that a discussion and a handshake were good enough to go on. My grandmother often voiced her misgivings about these arrangements, but Gramps wasn't one to say no to a family in need of water.

It wasn't so much that Nana minded him doing the work. She was proud of her industrious husband. It was just that, in those days, it was awful hard to get paid for what you did. But Gramps assured her that she needn't worry, he was sure it would all work out in the end, and did she have any more of that good sugar-cream pie left over?

And it always did work out. Gramps would drill a well for a farmer in a neighboring county, and later in the week a whole basket of eggs would appear on the front doorstep, then another and another, until one day they'd just stop coming. The drilling was paid for, the debt fulfilled.

One morning, a dairy farmer showed up with a payment in the back of his Ford pickup. He pulled into the gravel drive, dropped the tailgate, and hefted onto his shoulder a whole side of freshly butchered beef. "I expect this ought to make us about even on that drilling," he said to my grandfather. Gramps, as always, agreed.

There wasn't much room in the house for a side of beef, but it was wintertime in Indiana, so the slab stayed fresh under moistened cheesecloth on the screened-in back porch. Each day, Nana would step out onto the cold porch, select a prime cut of meat, and carry it back into the kitchen to prepare for an evening feast. She guarded that meat like it was pure gold.

After a few days, Nana noticed that the cheese-cloth had been moved. She asked Gramps if he had touched the beef. He hadn't. "Well, then," she said, "somebody's been at our meat. Have you been latching that back door?" Once again, my grandfather told her not to worry. She probably had moved the cloth herself and had simply forgotten.

This went on for many days. Nana was certain that someone was taking their meat, and Gramps was just as sure she was imagining things. It wasn't until much later that we learned the real story. . . .

On the morning after Gramps set the meat out on the back porch, he noticed footprints in the snow leading up to the porch door. Curious, he followed the footprints to where they began. Soon the impressions in the snow led my grandfather to a house he recognized—the home of a neighboring widow woman with two young children. Her husband had died from wounds sustained in the Great War. Her brother had moved in to help support the family, but he was unable to find work. The children were hungry. Gramps quietly turned around and walked back home. He didn't say a word about it to anyone.

From then on, Nana would carefully check the latch on the back porch door each night to make sure it was secure. Then Gramps, after waiting for Nana to go to bed, would return to the porch and release the latch again.

Nana never knew about the family they were helping to feed that winter. If she had, she would have baked some pies, stopped by for a visit, and tried to help in the only way she knew how. But Gramps understood a man's pride, and he knew it was not the thing to do. It was better this way.

The truth is, I don't know any of this firsthand. I know the story of the beef on the porch from my father's telling. It was his father who'd followed the footprints that day and unlatched the door each night. I have asked my father to repeat the story many times over the years. I'm especially fond of it, because it conveys the spirit of a man who worked hard during the hardest of times, yet never lost compassion for his neighbors—and because that man happens to be my grandfather.

If I have expressed some measure of the pride in my father's voice when he tells this story and in my heart when I hear it, then I have told the story of the well driller well.

~Mary Jane Chew

A Love That Burns Eternal

When most love stories speak of flames, it is a description of passion. That makes this love story completely the same and totally different from all the others.

The love began at least a year earlier. The flames arrived on the day after Christmas.

At age nineteen, Brian was incredibly fit and dangerously handsome—a Keanu Reeves look-alike with a flawless dark complexion, a gift of his European, Thai, and Native American family tree. At work harvesting trees that cold December day, he took a short break, to grab some lunch and to warm his hands over a fire. Some nearby cedar really lit up the fire already burning in the small barrel. The kindling worked almost too well. Tempering the flames with a bucket of water seemed like a good idea.

Brian's supervisor was eating a sandwich when

he heard the explosion. Launching himself from the small trailer office, Dan Kloppman saw Brian at ground zero of a 25-foot fireball. Running hard to reach him, he watched as the youth, engulfed in flames, rolled on the ground and then lay still.

Kloppman rolled Brian on the ground, but the fire was hungry. He attacked the brutal flames with his own bare hands, ripping away burning clothing, searing his own flesh in the process—to no avail. He realized that the only way to save Brian was to leave him. He rushed to the shop for a blanket to smother the fire. It worked.

There was no time to wait for an ambulance; they were too far off the beaten path. Kloppman and his wife, Angelee, lifted Brian into their van and hurtled down the 15 winding miles separating them from the hospital. Kloppman gripped the steering wheel, shut out the agony of his own pain, and flew.

The emergency room of the local hospital could only stabilize Brian. Then they sped him off in an ambulance, sirens screaming, to Emanuel Burn Center, in Portland, Oregon, about 70 miles away.

His case was uncharted terrain for even the experienced doctors. Triple-layer, full-thickness burns covered more than 96 percent of Brian's body. No one before had entered the burn center this badly injured and survived.

But the young man's heart kept beating.

Surgery followed surgery, and a war was waged against infection. The surly assailant claimed one limb after the other, each amputation a calculated sacrifice made against the goal of saving his life. Odds for his survival were nonexistent. Still, one day slipped into the next, and hope reached a tiny shoot toward the sun.

All the while, the love of Brian's life hung suspended in the balance. The warm light of young love had faded to the cold fluorescents of a hospital corridor. The gentle touch of a perfect romance had given way to the hard reality of an imperfect, burn-scarred world.

But as each difficult day unfolded, it became evident that there would be one certain survivor of this ordeal—the love between Brian and his fiancée, Haley.

Then came the heart-wrenching day when a life-threatening infection demanded amputation of both of his hands and forearms. Afterward, when Haley came out of his room, she smiled a gentle, hopeful smile. She said she had been talking to him, hoping her voice would reach through his coma, and patting his shoulder through the cushion of bandages.

"It was just as good as holding his hand," she said. "It will be all right."

Brian regained consciousness to find he had lost both hands, both forearms, and his left foot at mid-calf. But that didn't change Haley's love for him.

She remembered how Brian had helped her learn to accept herself. Now Haley, in turn, took the first step in helping Brian to accept himself, to cope with the aftermath of his injuries. One of the first things she told him when he was fighting his way back to consciousness was a simple but poignant message: "I bought my wedding dress last Sunday."

Smiles are rare in that burn ward. Brian's was broad and genuine, and it carried him through more surgeries, the loss of part of his other foot, and blindness.

An epic love story was written in that smile.

Brian and Haley had their wedding day.

She was beautiful. It didn't matter that Brian couldn't see her. He felt her radiance. If he could have looked around, he would have seen a chapel literally filled to capacity with well-wishers, most with tear-stained faces.

Brian's father proudly pushed his son's wheelchair down the aisle. There at the altar the young groom sat in silent anticipation, smiling reverently as Haley walked the aisle toward him. The ceremony was full of music, wonder, and celebration. But nothing prepared the guests for the moments to come.

Silence filled the chapel as Brian's father, Mo, stepped to his son's side and helped him rise from his wheelchair to stand on prosthetic feet. When his bride-to-be rested her hand on his upper arm, Brian stood as a whole man, ready to wed the girl of his dreams, who had been by his side throughout a horrific nightmare.

Brian spoke his vows in measured tones, through lips that had been painfully stretched and surgically given a semblance of their former shape. Haley spoke her vows in the reverent way she always knew she would. Brian's father, who stepped in as best man, gently placed the wedding ring on Haley's finger.

The bride had a ring for the groom, too. It didn't matter that he no longer had a finger on which to place it. She had threaded the ring onto a chain, which she now placed lovingly around his neck.

Through it all, Brian stood. No knight in shining armor ever stood taller. When he kissed his bride, every heart in the audience skipped a beat. Then Brian and Haley turned, faced their guests, and smiling, walked down the aisle as man and wife.

It may sound simple. It wasn't. Brian walked down that long aisle on prosthetic feet, unable to see where he was going, guided by his new wife, Haley. He didn't make a single misstep.

Many words have been written about courage, about resolve, about overcoming adversity, about the healing power of love. Those testimonies would be incomplete without these two words: Brian and Haley.

~Christy Caballero

Of Needs and Wants

When I was thirteen, in 1967, I started hanging around with a handful of kids a grade older than I was. That year I learned to smoke and swear, and I quit the baseball team. The previous year, as a rookie, I had made the age twelve-to-thirteen All-Star team. In 1967, as a veteran, not only would I not make the all stars, but I would not care about it.

The revolutionary 1960s were swirling around me, offering an invitation to freedom, to experimentation, and to break away from the shackles of authority to boldly go my own way. I was poised for a summer of nothingness, happily wallowing in the idea of irresponsibility. That is, until I learned that my mother, in her infinite wisdom and foresight, had arranged for me to spend the summer mowing a fraternity lawn with her father—my grandfather, the ex-army officer.

"Now, Bob," he'd said, looking at me and my tattered tennis shoes on the first day of work, "what you really need is a good pair of work boots."

What I really need, I thought, is to be back in bed and not mowing a lawn the size of Arlington National Cemetery in 90-degree heat under the watchful eye of Sergeant Perfectionist.

The lawn job, you see, was not some here-and-gone task that I could complete in a spare couple of hours. It was a full-time job. I was expected to show up every day precisely at 0800 hours, whereupon I was to complete a list of jobs that my grandfather had compiled the previous night on three-by-five-inch index cards: mowing, edging, watering, weeding, fertilizing, sweeping, pruning, planting, trimming, painting, sanding, scraping, taping, chipping, and clipping.

For this, I was to be paid $1.50 an hour.

Boots? Get real, I wanted to tell the old man. It was bad enough that I had to spend my first summer as a teenager trying to scrape unwanted grass from sidewalk cracks. Did I also have to wear a ball and chain in the process? Boots were restricting and clunky. Worst of all, at least in the mind of a thirteen-year-old boy knocking on the door of Sixties coolness, boots looked dorky.

From the beginning, it was clear that my grandfather and I were separated by more than two generations—it was more like two universes. We saw the world differently. We saw the job differently. We saw proper work attire differently. He showed up each morning in a uniform that was part U.S. Army and part *Home & Garden*: well-pressed beige pants, cuffed; a long-sleeved shirt, usually buttoned at the top; an Oregon State University baseball cap; and, of course, boots. Well-oiled boots.

At age sixty-eight and retired, Benjamin Franklin Schumacher presided over the grounds of the hallowed Sigma Alpha Epsilon (SAE) fraternity at OSU, where he was treasurer and self-appointed Guardian of the Grounds. To him it was not just a fraternity. It was a block-wide, split-level shrine. Nearly half a century before, at what was then known as Oregon Agricultural College, he had joined the SAEs. After college he had continued to be involved in the fraternity and had become affectionately known around town as "Schu of '22." In the years after World War II, my father and uncle had also been OSU SAEs.

My grandfather didn't think of the fraternity grounds as a mere collection of grass, shrubs, and bark dust. It was sacred ground, where he reigned as high priest of pruning and peat moss, and I was his obedient acolyte—albeit, an acolyte in cutoffs and scruffy black Converse All Stars.

"Now, Bob," he'd say, "tell that daughter of mine that she should invest in some good boots for you.

Get the ones with the steel-tipped toes. They'll protect you."

Then he'd laugh his heh-heh-heh laugh, a kind of chuckle that sounded like a sputtering lawn mower that wouldn't turn off, even when you hit the stop button.

Yeah, yeah, yeah.

The fraternity sat on the corner of two fairly busy streets in the college town of Corvallis, providing all the more reason for General Schumacher to want the lawn kept billiard-table green, the sidewalks swept, the hedges trimmed, and the fruit in his beloved apple trees wormless. Needless to say, he wasn't all that pleased when I overfertilized the Harrison Street quadrant and the grass turned the color of beef stroganoff, or when, upon returning from a weekend camping trip, I realized I'd accidentally left on the sprinklers for three solid days. But as the days on the job turned into weeks on the job, I noticed something about the man: he never got angry with me.

"I'll tell ya, Bob, nobody's perfect," he said after the sprinkler incident. Rather than berating me for doing something wrong, he simply took whatever tool I had used inappropriately and showed me how to use it correctly. He never said much; I learned by watching him.

"When you do a task," he'd say, "do it as well as you can, even if nobody is watching. When you try to fix something and find yourself stuck, improvise; use your imagination. When you take out a weed, get the whole root or the guy will come back in a few weeks."

(He always talked as if the weeds were human and part of some top-secret military operation, as if dandelions had units and captains, and as if crabgrass devised intricate plans to invade and capture.)

He led; I followed. While I did my work, he did his—except when he did his work, he went at it with a certain enthusiasm I couldn't muster, as if he found a deeper purpose to the job than just mowing, weeding, and trimming. As the day heated up, he would sweat an old-man's sweat, sometimes pulling out a handkerchief from his back pocket and wiping his forehead and neck, but never complaining.

"Work before play," he'd say. "Work before play."

One day, when I was changing the southeast sprinklers, a guy in a car turning onto Harrison Street rolled down his window and said, "Hey, looks great."

After he drove on, I looked over the landscaping and realized the man was right. It did look great. I realized people actually noticed the job we were doing. I realized, as deeply as a thirteen-year-old can realize, that I was part of something. Something good.

Gradually, I started to care about how the SAE grounds looked almost as much as my grandfather did. I learned to raise the wheels of the mower on uneven ground to prevent the blade from leaving scars. When an adjustment lever snapped off one of our rotating sprinkler heads, I learned to improvise with a paper clip. And when it came to weeds, I not only went after individual roots, I flushed out entire platoons.

For three summers I helped my grandfather take care of the SAE yard and came to believe that ours was the best-kept fraternity or sorority in Corvallis— maybe in the entire world. In the process, I learned a lot more than how to keep grass green, sidewalks swept, and trees trimmed. I learned that work was good and honorable. That what something looked like on the outside said a lot about what it was like on the inside. That there is a right way and a wrong way to do everything.

I also learned what it was to grow up and to care more and swear less. Just like the Gravenstein apple trees along 30th Street needed pruning to improve the fruit, so, too, had I needed some pruning, Schu had figured. And he had been right.

Finally, my stint at the SAE house ended. I made a career advancement and went to work raking beans and packing strawberries in a cannery at a mouth-watering salary of $2.50 an hour and with unbeatable fringe benefits: a pop machine and the aromas of a nearby Chinese restaurant.

One day in February of my sophomore year of high school, as I sat in Mrs. Shaw's English class, an office worker brought me a pink-slip message. "Your grandfather is waiting for you in the office," it read. The possibilities swirled in my mind as I hurried down the hall, heart pounding: my father is dead; my mother is dead. But, it turned out, nobody was dead.

"Now, Bob," my grandfather said, "I've arranged to take you out of school for a short time."

I asked why.

"Let's just say I have a little birthday surprise for you," he said and laughed his heh-heh-heh laugh.

We got into his gold Oldsmobile, which was roughly the size of the USS *Teddy Roosevelt*, and drove a mile down Buchanan Street to a one-stop shopping store, with me slumped low in the seat so nobody would see me. I couldn't figure out what was going on, so I just followed him into the store and eventually to the sporting goods section.

Some kids get cars on their sixteenth birthday. Some get stereos or ten-speed bikes or skis or skateboards. But in 1970 when I turned sixteen, my grandfather cared far too much about me to give me something I wanted. Instead, he gave me something I needed.

"Now, Bob," he said, "take your pick," gesturing toward a huge display of work boots, the kind with steel-tipped toes.

~Bob Welch

A Special Present

My eleventh birthday was just a week away the day we arrived at the refugee camp that bleak and cold November of 1947. My grandparents, who were raising me, and I had lived through the ravages of World War II, and then the Soviet occupation of our country, Hungary. The new communist regime was using terrorist tactics against the people who resisted the government, and because my grandfather was one of those resistors, we had fled with only the clothes on our backs. Our new home would be the "displaced persons camp" in Spittal, Austria.

To frightened, cold, and hungry refugees like ourselves, the camp was a blessing. We were assigned our own little cardboard-enclosed space in a barrack, fed hot cabbage-and-potato soup, and given warm clothes donated by caring people from countries like the United States of America. The Lord had seen us through some tough times; we had much to be thankful for. Though we had left behind our house, our friends, our homeland, and all our possessions, we were alive and safe and still had each other. We had left in a hurry in the middle of the night with virtually no money; even if my grandfather had managed to flee with a few *pengos* (Hungarian small currency) in his pocket, they would not have gone far in Austria. Given these circumstances, I had put any thought of birthday presents out of my mind.

My grandmother was the only mother I had ever known, and I loved her with all my heart. Still, I sometimes ached for my mother, who had died suddenly of pneumonia when I had been only a few weeks old, while my young father was away at war. Grandmother had stepped in to take over my care, and she and Grandfather had become my parents.

Grandmother was short and slightly plump, and had the bluest eyes I'd ever seen. Grandfather called them cornflower blue. He said he'd fallen in love with those eyes the first time he'd looked into them, and I always wished that my eyes were that color. Only thirty-six years old at the time of my birth, my grandmother could easily have passed for my birth mother. The war had aged her, however, and by the time she reached Austria at age forty-seven, streaks of gray had dulled her once lustrous, chestnut-brown hair, which she always wore in a little bun at the nape of her neck.

Before the war intensified, my birthdays had been grand celebrations with many cousins in attendance and gifts of toys, books, and clothes. Grandmother had always made me a *dobos torta*, a huge torte made with no fewer than a dozen eggs that was filled with a buttery custard and draped in a caramelized topping. The dobosh torta, which I always called a "drum cake" because it resembled a drum, was sinfully rich and delicious. Even now just thinking about it makes my mouth water.

The last purchased gift I had received had been for my eighth birthday, in 1944. By then, the war had intensified in Hungary, and times were hard, money was scarce, and survival was the primary goal. Yet, my grandparents had somehow managed—probably by hocking something—to buy me a book that year. And, oh, it was a wonderful book full of the humorous adventures of a girl my age, and I loved it. In fact, *Cilike's Adventures* had transported me from the harshness of the real world, where warplanes buzzed and bombs could come whistling out of the sky at any moment, to a make-believe world of laughter and fun. I remember carrying the book with me everywhere, even into bomb shelters.

After 1944, my birthday presents were usually

crocheted or knitted items, thanks to my grandmother's deft fingers, but there was always a present. On the eve of my eleventh birthday, feeling quite displaced in the refugee camp, I tried to resign myself to the reality: that there would be no party, no drum cake, and no birthday present this year.

The morning of my birthday I awoke early in our cardboard cubicle. Through the tiny window high on the cement wall, I noticed the gray, overcast sky. I lay there on my little cot beneath the scratchy horsehair blanket and thought about being eleven. I wondered what my mother would have thought of me. Why, I was almost grown up, and I resolved to act accordingly when my grandparents awoke. I didn't want them to feel badly about not being able to give me a present. I dressed quickly and tiptoed out as quietly as possible.

I ran across the dirt road, making fresh tracks in the newly fallen snow, to the women's bathroom and shower barracks. Even though it was chilly in there, I took my time washing and combing my hair. I kept looking at myself in the faded mirror over the cement sink, trying to see if I looked different now that I was eleven. But all I saw was a young girl with a thin face, long light-brown hair, and big blue eyes (though not cornflower blue, as I wished) staring back at me—nothing different from the day before.

Finally, I forced my feet forward and returned to our quarters; it was time to get the day over with.

"Good morning!" Grandfather's booming voice greeted me as soon as I walked in. "Happy birthday, sweetheart!"

"Thank you, but I'd just as soon forget about birthdays from now on," I replied, squirming in his generous hug. "After all, I'm practically a grownup now."

"When you get to be my age, you can think about forgetting birthdays," Grandmother said, walking over and taking me in her arms. "But you're much too young for that. Besides, who would I give this present to if we just forgot about your birthday?"

"Present?"

Dumbfounded, I watched her reach under the cot and pull something out of a brown bag stored there.

"Happy birthday, angel," she said, her eyes moist as she handed me the gift. "It's not much of a present, but I thought you might enjoy the company of an old friend on your eleventh birthday."

I felt like I was dreaming, for there in my hand I held my beloved old book.

"My *Cilike's Adventures*! But I thought it was left behind with our other things," I said, hugging the book close to me.

"Well, it almost was. But I knew how much you loved that book, and I couldn't bear to leave it behind. So I grabbed it along with my prayer book and stuck them in my coat pockets," Grandmother said. "Happy birthday again, Edesem. I'm sorry it's not a new book, but I hope you like having it back again."

"Oh, Grandmother, thank you! Thank you! I'm so very happy to have *Cilike* back," I said, hugging her again, tears streaming down my face. "This is the best birthday present ever!"

It really was. Because on my eleventh birthday, I realized I was blessed with a wonderful grand-mother/mother, whose love would always see me through. And I knew the mother I'd never known was smiling down on us from heaven.

~*Renie Szilak Burghardt*

Drywall in the Time of Grief

I can tell you all about grief, but I'd rather talk about drywall and the way mud is spackled across the tape in smooth flowing runs until it disappears, its edges morphed into gray flat evenness. How it must turn dry until it is sanded again and more mud applied, each layer growing even with the wall it conjoins. I can tell you about texturing and priming and bringing an ugly thing to beauty and completion. Only then can I take your hand and tell you about sorrow and the need for busy hands.

When my husband of thirty-one years died suddenly of a heart attack, his death not only left a hole in my heart, it also left a hole in my kitchen wall. It was as tall and wide as the refrigerator it once held, an ugly maw to the decrepit room full of boots and tools behind it.

Once, for a gradation party for one of our sons,

we framed the space around it with molding and hung a curtain in front. "For when we remodel," my husband had said. But that was not likely. The wind came under the back door and broken floor. Its cold breath stirred the curtain. Money wasn't at hand. It was never done.

So there I was, fifty-five and widowed and as lonely as the First Day, with no one to turn to. A newly framed garage leaned dangerously towards the neighbor's yard, and the back fence had fallen down. There was that hole in my kitchen wall. To add insult to injury, I got robbed.

An empty house is a widow's bane, easily vacated on the flimsiest reason or timed for late arrival from work or outings so that you can just go to bed and be done with the day. There is no one to greet you, no one to ask about your day or grouse about life's infractions. There is only silence, a living thing that grows until it grips you like its prey.

I escaped from the house the very next day after my husband's death, compelled to drive to Bellingham Bay, where the two of us had walked my husband's chocolate Lab on the beach every day. I took his jeep and cried all the way through town and the full length of the beach, until I could no longer see through the blur of tears. I finally stopped, looking for a sign that I wasn't alone. I thought of the bald eagles we'd seen only the day before. I asked God to send me one, and He did. One snap of a finger, and an eagle flew out of nowhere, its wing-tips stretched out and tickling the clear morning air. It came toward me, and then veered away, its white tail like a trapezoid flag.

Over the next three days, I saw bald eagles all the time—over my house, at the funeral home, and at the beach again. I also saw red-tailed hawks, rough-legged hawks, peregrines, and herons. My Native American friends said that was good. My husband's spirit was speaking to me. It gave me solace most of the time, but I still had to go home.

I sought comfort and advice. The best didn't come from well-meaning friends or family; it came from those who had faced the same trial. Only a bereaved knows the bereaved, I discovered. It's as though we had all stepped into an exclusive room no others could see.

"Welcome to the silent sisterhood," one widow said.

"Time does heal, but first it'll get worse before it gets better," said another.

"It took me five years."

"You'll never get over it, but you will go on."

"Keep busy."

I decided to keep busy.

A week after the robbery and a scant month after my husband died, a member of my church came to check out my flagging door. It sagged on its pins, its middle sections weak and rotten. The lock didn't hold either.

"Uh," Claude said as he pushed on it. "Looks pretty bad."

After tinkering around the frame, he announced he was going to remove the door and take it home. "The panels are bad, but the rest of the door is firm. Besides, a new solid door is costly."

In the meantime, he would nail a board over the opening.

That's when I pointed out the hole in my kitchen wall. Could there be any help on that? "I'll do it myself if someone will show me how," I said.

Claude turned and smiled. He'd see what he could do about that.

Two days later I came home from work to find the door back in its place and Claude working on the threshold. It was still rotten at the bottom of the wall, and the wind still came through, but a rolled towel could take care of that. I tried the door. It clunked when it shut. It was as solid as an iron gate. Then I looked at the wall to the left. Claude had set in a new sheet of drywall and taped it.

"Look on the other side."

I went into the kitchen. A sheet of drywall hung where the maw had been before.

Now the work would begin.

Grief cannot be hurried. It cannot be forced. It doesn't go away just because the rest of the world thinks there is a certain number of days to finish it up or because tears at odd junctures are unsettling. Grief has its own timeline, its own rhythm.

Drywall is like that. It takes patience and concentration. And it takes time.

It also takes the proper tools. Claude gave me two: a wide spackling knife and a preprimed board scrap that was smooth and even. He also showed me how to scoop the spackle from its pot and work it with the knife upon the board until it was smooth as icing on a cake.

Back and forth. Back and forth. Slab a glob on the tape, then push so the blade splays out and spreads it thin. Wipe excess on the edge of the board and start again.

Soon the knife flowed across the tape until the edges disappeared. I could have ended it there and called it done, but a wall takes time. Old must flow into new until it is one.

I learned to wait.

Each night I would come home from work to the empty house, dreading its echoes, and to a dog who worried that I, too, would leave her. But after changing my clothes, I'd go to the wall and sand down the rough edges of yesterday's work. Taking up the board and knife, I would start anew, adding a new layer to the last. When I was done, I'd let it dry until the next day.

By the end of the week, it was finished. The tape had disappeared, and the wall felt smooth to the touch, with no distinction between the old to the new. I sanded one more time, added texture, again waiting for it to set up. I primed it and eventually painted the new wall and the entire kitchen.

Then I started to work on the bare drywall concealing the backside of the old maw. Once again I covered the tape with spackle, sanded it, and added more mud until the new piece flowed into the old. I textured, primed, and painted, and I learned to use molly screws to put up some shelves.

I moved upstairs, tore out ancient rugs and painted again. Busy hands to heal, to transform.

I am at peace now. It *has* taken nearly five years. Though I can still cry on a dime when I see a bald eagle fly across my path, read a handwritten note of my husband's, or celebrate alone one of our three son's achievements, I am happy most of the time. I have left the "us" and "ours" of my life and moved into the "mine" and "me," carrying those precious thirty-one years with me.

The house feels new. The rotten walls at the back are gone and replaced with new solid ones—all of which I've painted. I have gutters and gardens, and this fall a new furnace will warm the house completely for the first time in the many years I've lived here. Holding it all up is a new foundation of historic-looking blocks that has replaced sandstone rocks and bricks. In a sense, all my grief is cleaned and spackled away.

There are new cracks in the walls, but this comes naturally from a century-old house settling onto its new foundation. I will come home at night, and after sipping iced tea or even wine, I will take my spackling knife and board in hand and fill each crack with patience, love, and care.

~Janet Oakley

Listen to Your Heart

I teach a bilingual kindergarten class in Oakland,
California. One Monday morning while talking
with my students about the calendar and birthdays,
I noticed that two of my students, Juan and Cynthia,
had a shared birthday on Friday of that week. I informed both Juan's and Cynthia's moms that they
could bring in cupcakes to celebrate their children's
birthdays at school.

I always try to recognize each of my students'
birthdays. Not only is it important for children
to learn this vital information—when and where
they were born, and how old they are—it also
helps develop self-esteem. By the end of the day on
Wednesday, I'd heard nothing back from either Juan's
or Cynthia's parents, and I wondered whether either
intended to bring in a birthday treat for the kids. On
Thursday, I asked Juan and Cynthia about it, but

they didn't know anything about their parents' plans to celebrate their birthdays at school. Both children, however, were very excited about having a birthday party the next day in class.

I had several errands to run after work that day and decided to pick up cupcake makings for Juan and Cynthia's party. Only after I was home and settled did I realize I'd forgotten to stop at the market to buy cake and frosting mix. Exhausted, as one tends to get trying to keep up with a classroom of twenty kindergartners every day, I decided to lie down on the couch for a short rest before going to the store and making the cupcakes. I awoke with a start hours later! By that time it was too late to go to the store, so I stumbled off to bed.

I awoke before the alarm the next morning and decided to go in early to catch up on some work. Then I remembered the cupcakes. First I thought, *Oh, I'll bet one of the mothers made them*, which was quickly replaced by a stronger and very distinct thought, *No, you were supposed to make them*. Frankly, I was a little upset; I didn't want to feel obligated to make cupcakes every month or for every child. But I was mostly upset at myself for not making the cupcakes. Most parents did offer or agree to my suggestion to bring in a treat to celebrate their children's birthdays with their classmates. This time, my suggestion had been followed by silence. That silence spoke very loudly to me as I approached the Mexican bakery on my drive to school.

Now, I knew the bakery only made birthday cakes on special order ahead of time. Plus, I had a sum total of five dollars in my purse that had to last until payday, and I didn't really want to spend it on Mexican sweetbread, which isn't exactly a birthday cake in the minds of five-year-olds, anyway. If I did spend the money on a cake, I wouldn't be able to buy myself lunch, which I normally packed but had forgotten that day. Still, I felt compelled to drive to that bakery, the whole way thinking to myself: *Why am I going there? I can't spend my last five dollars before payday on cake. Besides, they have no cake.* But something inside me shouted, *Go!*

Before I knew it, I was standing in the bakery, looking for cake I knew wasn't there. Then I noticed they had four large slices of cake for a dollar apiece. I bought all four pieces, leaving me with exactly one dollar for lunch. I placed the white bag with the cake next to me on the passenger seat and carefully drove the three blocks to school. After parking the car in the street, I walked around to the other side to get the cake and my school bag. As I opened the car door, I looked down and saw a five-dollar bill, folded in half, lying on the curb next to my car. I picked up the damp bill, thinking someone must have dropped it the night before. *Wow!* I thought. Now the kids would have cake and I'd have lunch, too.

When I got into the classroom, I put the four pieces of cake side by side and looked for some candles. I found a box with exactly five pink ones and five blue ones. With the candles, the "cake" looked pretty convincing. I teach morning kindergarten; the children arrive at eight o'clock and have breakfast in the cafeteria, so we don't usually have snacks. But I try to keep paper plates, napkins, and plastic spoons on hand for special treats, such as on holidays and birthdays. I was distressed to find only a tiny stack of paper plates left in the cupboard, certain there wouldn't be enough, but there were exactly twenty. Then I counted the plastic spoons left in the bowl: only nineteen. I rummaged around in the cupboard and found a box with a single spoon left in it. All I needed were napkins, which I was relieved to find we had plenty of.

My students piled in, put away their backpacks and coats, and dropped their homework into the homework box. The day went well. After story time, we did the calendar, and I told them, "Today we are celebrating the double birthdays of Juan and Cynthia."

I brought out the cake and lit the candles, and then we sang "Happy Birthday" to the birthday kids. Cynthia and Juan beamed with happiness; their faces glowing brighter than the candles. The birthday boy and girl enthusiastically blew out their candles, and the children sat patiently while I quickly sliced each of the four pieces into five little slivers. It was just enough: all twenty of my students had come to class that day.

After the children finished eating their snack, I stood by the trash bin to make sure the plates, spoons, and napkins all went into the container. Juan was still smiling when he tossed in his plate and said, "Teacher, I never had a birthday party before!"

As I watched Juan trot away, still grinning from ear to ear and with a new little bounce to his step, tears came to my eyes. When Cynthia came up moments later, I asked her if she'd ever had a birthday party before.

"No," she said, and then beamed her brightest smile. "But I loved my birthday today! Thank you, Teacher."

I later learned, after talking with their parents, that our simple celebration had, indeed, been both Cynthia's and Juan's first birthday party.

Some unseen force within me had directed me

to a bakery that normally sold only preordered cakes and to spend my last few dollars on four slices of cake to split among twenty five-year-olds. Had I listened to logic, Juan and Cynthia might still be waiting for their first birthday party—and I might not have learned the most valuable kindergarten lesson of all: to listen to my heart.

~Susanmarie Lamagna

A Daughter's Trust

It was the day of the solar eclipse, the last day of a great vacation, and my nine-year-old daughter and I were caught in quicksand. We'd been walking along the beach when the tide suddenly changed, and we started to sink. Larissa looked at me terror-stricken, movie scenes of quicksand gobbling people up no doubt flashing in her mind.

We had journeyed to Costa Rica for a rare treat: father and daughter alone together on an adventure. I'd wanted to share a different world with her and for her to experience a unique environment in its natural state. I'd selected a hotel on a less-traveled area on the Pacific coast and had taken her to places and shown her things that most tourists never see.

Our hotel, while reasonably elegant, was far from being the typical beach resort. The area was remote, with few stores and tourist attractions. Our last plane had even had to buzz over the almost abandoned runway to chase off the goats before we could land. We had explored the capital city of San José and had ridden the mountain train down to the coast. We had wandered through the cloud forests and the banana plantations by the sea. The eclipse would be the highlight of our trip—or so I thought.

On our last full day in Costa Rica, we both awoke feeling refreshed and happy. I hoped for the gift of a cloud-free sky, as on a clear day at that location, so close to the equator, the eclipse would be clearly visible. Since the sun wasn't due to disappear until 2:05 that afternoon, we decided to take one last, slow walk on the beach.

Even the beach had a primitive feel. Instead of the unrelenting expanses of manicured sand so often found in resorts, it featured large rocky areas with tidal pools and outcroppings of coral. While this made for a more interesting beach, it was tough on our city feet, so we took grateful advantage of every patch of sand. We had stopped on just such a spot to study the life in a tidal pool when the tide suddenly changed. The effect was swift and greatly magnified by the shape of the bay, and the ocean began to rush toward the shoreline in huge funnels.

At the same time, we began to sink into the sand beneath us. I turned my attention from watching the crabs and minnows to watching Larissa. The quicksand had barely covered her ankles when she looked up at me.

"Dad," she asked, worry straining her voice, "are we in quicksand?"

"Why, yes dear, we are." I nodded and smiled.

She studied my face. I looked away, as if sinking in quicksand were the most ordinary of events, careful to watch her only out of my peripheral vision. Puzzled at first, she was now giving the situation careful consideration. Soon, she broke into a radiant smile. Then she asked me a question I will always cherish.

"Well, Dad," she inquired cheerfully, "why aren't we worried?"

Not, "Why aren't *you* worried?" but, "Why aren't *we* worried?"

Her question, along with her curious but no longer troubled reaction to the quicksand sucking at our legs, told me all I needed to know.

So I told her.

I explained that tidal pockets of quicksand are almost always shallow. Even if we did get caught in deep quicksand, we could simply bend over backward at our knees, spreading our weight over a larger surface, and eventually work our way free. Unless we were foolish enough to remain standing erect until the ground swallowed us up, we could easily float on a mixture of sand and water while we gradually backstroked our way to safety.

As I expected, the pool of quicksand we were standing in was shallow, and our downward descent stopped well before it reached my daughter's knees. At that point, though we did have some difficulty working free of its embrace, we did not have to resort to the sandy backstroke.

The eclipse turned out to be spectacular, and as a bonus, the sky blossomed with stars before the sun came out from behind the moon. Yet, precious as the memory of witnessing such a sight on the Costa Rican coast with my daughter on my shoulders is, it is eclipsed by the gift I received from Larissa's simple question: the proof of my daughter's unfailing trust.

~David Kirkland

A Heaping Helping
of Thanksgiving

She was a horrible waitress. Never got anybody's order right. Always screwed up something on the customers' bills, sending them complaining to the manager. There were stains all over her gaudy pink uniform and runs in her stockings. Her bright-orange, Brillo-pad hair and pickle-like nose planted in the middle of her oval face made her look just like that adorable Muppet, Fozzy the Bear. Only, our Fozzy wasn't quite so adorable.

On Thanksgiving night, when no one else wanted to work, only Fozzy and I manned the wait stations, serving molded turkey shavings and ice cream scoops of mashed potatoes to the clusters of senior citizens who stumbled in out of the brisk November cold. Fozzy and I had never talked much, and that night was no exception. As Christmas carols blasted out of the diner's Muzak system, Fozzy hummed along, off-key, all night. Although I tried to share her enthusiasm, I had too much on my mind to be able to really feel cheerful.

My college tuition was due, and I was hard-pressed for cash. My father's business was in disarray, and he was considering filing for bankruptcy. After my parents' divorce, my mother had moved to an oceanfront condominium way beyond her means, which she had later put up for sale. In the entire year it had been on the market, however, not one person had made her an offer. My life felt out of control, and I had no one to turn to. Given their financial difficulties, how could I possibly remind my parents of their long-standing offer to help pay for my college tuition?

I'd been slaving away at the diner for nearly a year, trying to save up enough for my first semester at the local state university, and I had finally reached my goal. Then, just that morning, my car had refused to start. The mechanic had said that the entire electrical system was faulty and that it would cost more than $500 to fix it.

"Five hundred dollars?" I heard someone say. I blinked my eyes and stared into Fozzy's solemn face.

"And just when you were so close to starting college, too. Not a very happy Thanksgiving, is it?"

Had I really just admitted all of my troubles aloud? Had Fozzy actually listened?

Impossible as it seemed, there we were, nestled quietly over two cups of mud-like diner coffee, killing time while the last few customers of the evening wandered out into the miserable cold.

"Thank you," I said humbly, feeling a lump in my throat at having negatively judged Fozzy. "I didn't mean to go on like that. Thank you for listening."

"Well now," she sighed. "It sounds to me like not much listening has been going on in your family these days, with everybody rushing around with their own problems. Sometimes a friendly ear can change the way you think about things."

She was right. Pouring out my troubles, things I hadn't even told my best friends, had left me feeling like I'd just had a restful night's sleep.

"Listen," she said later, as we clocked out. "I've been trying to sell my old car for weeks. It's in good shape. Now, it's not exactly a babe magnet, but I'm only asking three hundred for it. That's less than it would take to fix your car. Maybe the money you'd save would round out what you need for tuition."

"And then some," I gasped, leaping at the offer like a little kid.

We sat quietly on the way to her apartment, the only two on the bus, everyone else busy celebrating the holiday with family and friends. I thought of my mom, attending the annual gala Thanksgiving dinner party at the country club, despite her having had to borrow money from my grandmother to pay for the ticket. I thought of my dad, working double-time at his company, trying to straighten things out. Neither of them had bothered to ask me what I'd be doing for the holiday.

Fozzy's car was an eight-year-old Honda with a little rust and nearly new tires. The paint was faded, and the interior was worn, but the engine turned over in an instant and purred like a kitten. The car had more than 100,000 miles on it, but it was in better shape than the car I had been planning to fix. I couldn't believe my good luck.

"The paperwork is upstairs," said Fozzy. "I won't keep you long, I'm sure you have big plans for tonight."

Yeah, right.

I watched sadly as Fozzy slowly waddled away from me. I noticed for the first time that she favored one leg and that the soles of her cheap shoes looked old and worn. The halls of her building were dark and quiet, and I picked up enough clues to determine that Fozzy wasn't exactly walking into a festive apartment, either.

Fozzy's smile filled the corridor as she opened her

door, welcoming me in. While she fumbled through a desk for the car's paperwork, I sat on a threadbare couch and looked around her modest one-bedroom apartment. The room was clean and cozy, and the table was set with a paper tablecloth featuring turkeys and pilgrims. Turkey candles and pilgrim salt-shakers rounded out her festive holiday decorations.

"Oh, I'm sorry," I said, noticing that the table had been set for two. "I didn't realize you were expecting company."

Fozzy smiled sadly, looking at her feeble attempts to bring the holiday into her home.

"Oh no. That is just habit. Ever since my husband died six years ago, I can't stand to see a table set for one. I just leave out two plates, so people don't go feeling sorry for me. I don't even know why I bothered this year," she said.

While Fozzy signed the title, I looked around the room at her shabby furniture and homemade curtains. Scattered about were photographs of several young men and women in various celebratory poses: graduations, promotions, birthdays. Younger versions of Fozzy stood nearby, smiling proudly. *Where were her children this holiday night?* I wondered.

Just then my stomach rumbled. I'd been too upset all night to even think about food, but suddenly I was starving.

"Listen," I said, pulling out the wad of ones and fives I had earned during my shift at the diner. "I had a pretty good night. Why don't we order some take-out, so your nice table here doesn't go to waste. My treat. It's the least I can do to thank you for bailing me out like this."

Fozzy couldn't find the phone fast enough. "Do you like Chinese?"

Later, as Fozzy showed off the interior of the car and its impressive features, most of which no longer worked, and I noticed the stains on her threadbare uniform, I felt an aching in my heart. Her kind and generous gesture had afforded me the opportunity to finally start college on time. Classes would start soon, I would move away from home, and once settled, find a cushy job on campus and start the process of financial aid and student loans. My long, hard nights of dishing up buttered carrots and creamed spinach were nearing an end. I wondered how many long, hard years Fozzy would have to work before she could finally retire.

As I drove away in my new used car toward a brighter future made possible by the kind act of a near stranger, I ran over a bump and the faulty glove box door fell open. Inside I spotted a thin envelope, which I opened and read at a stoplight. Once I finished reading it, I had to pull over until my tears dried up and I could see the road again.

"Thank you for the first Thanksgiving I've celebrated in six years," said a quickly scrawled note on a scrap of paper. "This isn't much, just the tips I made tonight. Maybe you can buy one of your textbooks on me. Thanks again, Mavis."

Mavis, I thought, pulling back onto the road. All those nights working together and it had been there on her nametag the whole time—if I'd only looked: Mavis.

I counted the money in the envelope. There was enough for not one, but two, textbooks. There was also enough for a brand-new uniform for Mavis. I couldn't wait to give it to her.

~Rusty Fischer

In the Arms of Grace

The powerful earthquake hit our home in the early hours of January 17, 1994, jolting my husband and me awake and nearly tossing us from our bed. Our instant response was to run and get our two sons, Dustin, seven, and Jonathan, four, who shared a room with twin beds at the other end of the house. This task seemed nearly impossible, however, as the giant tremors repeatedly threw us to the floor of our upstairs bedroom.

All electrical power in the area immediately went out, and my husband and I found ourselves scrambling across the house in total darkness punctuated only by the light we could see from the windows caused by exploding transformers on nearby hilltops. My husband grunted in pain as a tall wooden bookcase fell and gashed his right leg.

"Go on, go get the boys," he yelled through gritted teeth.

I heard him pushing the bookcase off his leg, then the deafening sounds of glass shattering throughout the house. An aftershock knocked me to my knees before I reached the boys' bedroom. A metallic taste abruptly filled my mouth, and I realized I had bitten my tongue.

The shaking stopped, and everything became eerily quiet as I peered into my sons' shadowy bedroom. By now accustomed to the darkness, I could make out that all three of their bookcases had toppled into the center of the room, having narrowly missed their beds. My older son's bed was closer to the door, so I reached him first after crawling over the debris. Dustin was shaking with fear, but he was huddled safely beneath the covers.

"It's an earthquake," I said quietly. "Stay under the covers until I get Jonathan, and then we'll all go downstairs together."

I turned toward my younger son's bed and froze. Just then, I heard my husband gasp in the doorway behind me. A moment later he was by my side. The tall chest of drawers had tipped over onto my younger son's bed. We could see his pillow peeking out from beneath the fallen dresser. To make matters worse, two tall plaster giraffes weighing 25 pounds each, gifts to the boys from a family friend, had both fallen into the center of Jonathan's bed, breaking in half from the force of their fall.

Fearing what we would find under the dresser and broken giraffes, my husband and I quickly shoved the heavy dresser off the bed. In the instant before turning back toward the bed, I closed my eyes and said a quick prayer:

"God, I've always prayed only to thank you, never feeling I needed your help. Now, please God, I need a miracle."

I opened my eyes and saw a smashed but empty pillow. We pulled the plaster giraffes off the bed and searched the bedclothes. Jonathan was nowhere in sight. Tears filled my eyes, and I hugged my husband, saying, "He's here somewhere, and he's okay. I know it."

Another strong aftershock struck, and we realized we had to find Jonathan and all get out of there quickly. My husband didn't have his glasses on, so I told him to take Dustin outside and that I would continue to search for Jonathan. Then we heard a strange noise that seemed to come from Jonathan's bed. We crept back to the bed and heard coughing coming from inside the small headboard cupboard where Jonathan stored his favorite toys and books.

There, impossibly tucked inside the tiny cubby of the headboard, lay Jonathan, tired but unharmed. My husband scooped him up, and I grabbed Dustin. The four of us made our way downstairs as the house continued to fall apart around us. On the way, I remembered to grab our emergency earthquake bag from the downstairs closet. As soon as we got outside we smelled smoke. The only light we could see came from a glow to the north, which we later learned was caused by gas explosions.

We climbed into my station wagon, which was parked at the curb, and caught our breath for a few minutes. We dressed the kids in sweat suits from the emergency bag and handed out snacks and water. With our family safe and warm, we decided to check up on our neighbors.

First, though, I ran back inside the unstable house for my husband's glasses and then again for supplies. After seeing to our neighbors, our greatest concern became whether Los Angeles still existed. We hoped that we were close to the epicenter, which would mean that the extensive damage around us would probably be the worst of it. We later learned that we were only about a mile from the epicenter of the Northridge quake.

When morning finally came, my husband and

I looked at our utterly destroyed house. Both chimneys had fallen, the windows were broken, and the downstairs was flooded from a broken pipe. We had only lived there for four months and had put every penny we had into buying and redecorating the place. Now, it all lay in ruins. But our faith in God remained firmly in place; we were deeply thankful that all four of us were alive and well.

Over the course of the following year, we lost both our home and a separate rental property to foreclosure because we hadn't carried earthquake coverage. Yet friends and family took us in, clothed and fed us, and made us feel welcome. My husband and I became less concerned about material things and money. We both spent more time enjoying our children and each other.

Today, we live in another nice home in Northridge, and our sons attend great schools. Every day, we try to perform a simple kindness or service to family, friends, or strangers. We feel blessed by God and humbled enough to need and accept his help.

When we finally felt Jonathan could discuss the earthquake without suffering additional trauma, we asked him why he had crawled into the headboard.

He thought about it for a moment and then said, "I didn't crawl in. The beautiful lady put me in."

We were stunned.

"The beautiful lady?" I asked.

"Yeah. She smelled pretty, like you, Mom. And she had wrinkles all over her."

That was all Jonathan would ever say about his experience.

To this day, we have never questioned the miracle of our son's survival. Now and then I say a prayer for the mysterious beautiful lady, whoever she was—the figment of a small boy's imagination or a special messenger some might call an angel. Through her, God had protected our son from harm and had helped give us a better understanding of our purpose here on earth. Real or imagined, she changed our lives, and we believe in her.

~Lynda Kudelko Foley

Maddie's Rose

The first house my husband and I bought was a cookie-cutter colonial in one of northern Virginia's countless subdivisions.

Though Virginia is predominantly a rural state, developers of the bedroom communities that had sprouted up almost overnight like so many patches of identical mushrooms, just outside the nation's capital, had stripped the land of much of its wild finery. Often they would build four or more houses on a single acre, never mind the fact that sometimes the windows of one house would peer directly into the windows of another. It was in one of these plain boxes that I grew in ways I never would have dreamed possible.

During our protracted period of house hunting, I would reject one house after another for carrying the stamp of another person's personality. I'm sure that after a while our realtor wanted to hang me by the handiest Laura Ashley curtain tieback, but I was adamant. I would know "the house" when I saw it. And I did.

When I first walked through the door of the house we would buy, the crisp winter sun seemed to welcome me, streaming joyfully through the high windows in the cathedral foyer. The decor was white and gold, making for a clean and uncomplicated design. I found the simple open floor plan soothing, and I knew that, here, I could expand in every direction.

After we had bought the house and spring was making itself felt in the air, I watched eagerly for the opportunity to plant my first garden. In pots on the dining room table, I started foxglove and columbine from seeds culled on our honeymoon in England. Such magnificent plans I had!

Mother Nature wasn't the only one bursting with new life that spring. I was pregnant with our first child and believed that no baby could ever have been more keenly anticipated than the one kicking furiously in my belly. With the days of morning sickness gone and the sun hanging ever longer in the sky, I used the extra hours to beat back the stubborn red Virginia clay. I bustled about the yard, striving to bring life to the hard soil that refused to hold water.

Since there were no worms in my garden, I traveled to my mother's place in North Carolina and transported jars and jars of the creatures. I became an extension of my garden, my nails chipped and stained with red clay, my dreams filled with mulch and peat and the constant rush of sprinklers.

The lot behind us was empty when we first moved in, an oversight the industrious builders eventually corrected. The undeveloped rectangle was overgrown with reminders of what the land had once looked like: thorny bushes, saplings, and the promise of a bumper crop of ragweed. The neighbors sighed with relief when the backhoe arrived to remove this blight from the civilized face of the community. I mourned the loss of that small vestige of wildness that had thumbed its nose at neatly clipped grass and greenhouse annuals in orderly rows.

The backhoe made fast progress, and soon all that remained of the unconquered square was a small corner. Drawn to the patch on the eve of its destruction, I sat among the doomed thorns and young trees, remembering my childhood in countryside that had looked remarkably similar to this tiny triangle of suburban wilderness. I remembered how thrilling each day of natural discovery had been as a child, finding raspberries on the sharp brambles and nests of hairless baby mice sheltered in the snarled grass. As

I studied the tangles of branches around me, I noticed in the soft green of pale new leaves the toothy three- and five-leaf patterns of roses. Astonished, I waddled to my garage as fast as I could and grabbed a shovel.

It was nasty, hard work, and my hands had the gouges to prove it. The vicious thorns, fighting my efforts to save them, sliced through the leather gloves I was wearing. But with a loud *pop* the roots finally gave, and I fell backward with a thump. A neighbor waved to me from her deck, most likely thinking that the hormones had gotten the best of me and I was in some kind of pregnancy-induced lunacy. Waving back, I grabbed up my prize and hurried to the front of my house, where a large hole was already waiting. I knew that time was of the essence in preventing the roots, deceptively delicate in spite of their heftiness, from drying out.

By that time, neighbors coming home from work were wandering over to see what I was doing, a regular practice on our cul-de-sac. The consensus over my new planting was that I had been out in the sun too long and that my husband had better take me inside and cool my fevered brow with a wet cloth and an iced tea. I insisted that the homely bramble was really a wild rose, a claim that was met with skeptical looks and derisive snorts. They no doubt feared that I'd taken the final leap over the edge of sanity, which might eventually lead to other questionable practices—such as placing pink flamingoes on my lawn and thereby damaging the market value of their precisely maintained homes.

Over the next few days, while the rose drooped pitifully, its leaves and stems limp with shock, I refused to admit defeat. I tended it as if it were a sick child, watering it carefully in the early morning and evening. Yet even my husband, who usually lovingly tolerated my frequent madnesses, expressed doubt that this one would pan out. But as humans so often do, he had underestimated Mother Nature's vigor. The supple branches soon regained their firmness and the leaves revived, darkening to a green so rich it seemed tinged with black.

The rose quickly covered the trellis I had placed hopefully behind it and went on to spread its glossy arms across the red brick front of the house. I trained it carefully between the windows, wary of the thorns that had already taken their pound of flesh from my hands. Each day I fondly tended my wild rose, mindful of where it had come from, determined not to stifle its fierce, feral beauty. Soon it bore an abundance of impossibly tiny buds, curled tight and green and almost hidden in the thriving foliage. I waited expectantly for the buds to open, checking each day for some sign to reward my diligence.

One afternoon, as breathtakingly flawless as only a May day can be, I left to give birth to our child. As I looked for the first time into the round blue eyes of my perfect daughter, I was filled with an overwhelming sense of utter ecstasy, then peace. We named her Madeleine.

When I arrived home with my small family, I was greeted by a magnificent surprise: The wild rose had at last opened its blossoms—in a riot of elegant pink blooms so pale they were almost white. The petite flowers were so profuse they practically obscured the green leaves. The rose's beauty was absolute and unspoiled, as fresh and pure as a new babe.

I no longer live in Virginia, but Maddie's rose still blooms in my heart—tangled and untamed and beautiful.

~Ella Magee

Rejoice the Ides of March

At seventeen, I was the oldest passenger on the train that fifteenth day of March 1939. The train, departing from Vienna, was carrying refugee children to Holland and England, a program sponsored by a Jewish organization in London. The other children ranged in age from seven to twelve. What set me apart was my age and that I was journeying to England on my own. What bound us together was the fact that we were all on the train for the same reason: we were fleeing the Holocaust. This was before Hitler's "final solution," which would snuff out the lives of so many, including my maternal grandfather and three of my aunts.

I was a young seventeen, sheltered and unworldly. Short and slight, I also looked younger than my years, so I blended in with the others. I carried a large brown suitcase in one hand and a book in the other. The pocket of my coat held only a slip of paper carrying a name and an address.

Perhaps twenty-five of us had boarded the train in Austria; our faces had flattened against the windowpanes as we strained for a farewell glimpse of our families. My mother, tiny but determined, pushed through the crowd, craning her neck and gesturing to me. I knew her sign language; she was telling me to make sure to wear my muffler. Her small, upturned face was knotted in anguish. When would she see me again? Somewhere in the crowd was my younger brother, Paul. Would we ever again lie next to each other in bed and read adventure stories together about the American West?

My father was also somewhere in the crowd. Only two months earlier, he had returned from Dachau, where he had been imprisoned for six weeks. He'd been released only because he had signed a sworn statement that he would leave Austria as soon as possible. An uncle in America, my father's brother, was preparing the affidavit that would save all our lives.

I was the first to leave—not for America, but for England, where a distant relative knew someone who could find work for me. At the time, families were being partitioned like occupied land. Staying alive had to take precedence over staying together.

When the train began to move and we were wrenched from our loved ones, the smaller children began to whimper. After a while, however, the motion of the train lulled them to sleep. Others reached into their backpacks for a chocolate bar or a kaiser roll with salami or cheese. One boy took a deck of cards from his pocket and began a game of rummy. A little girl, maybe seven years old, with a pale round face and dark bangs sat across from me. Her name was Liesel, and she quietly sobbed into a dainty embroidered handkerchief. She sobbed all the way to Holland.

I didn't converse with the others; I felt like an outsider. The children all wore identification on their lapels. Someone would be waiting for each child, eager to welcome him or her, to provide a home, to teach the language. I wore no identification; no one would be meeting me. All that was waiting for me was the possibility of some vague job in a strange country whose language I could not speak.

My memories of the journey are incomplete. I remember it seemed interminable. That I read my book and gazed out the window and dozed. That the moment we crossed the border out of Germany, two or three boys raised the window, turned their faces backward, and spat. I remember I felt alone and frightened. And hungry. My mother had packed a lunch for me, but I had eaten it hours earlier.

A few children got off in Holland. One of them was Liesel. I peered out the window, wondering if she was all right. An older woman with a smiling face was bending over her, taking her hand. Adults stood on the platform holding photographs and scanning faces, arms outstretched. The children hung back at first, and then cautiously inched toward their new families.

When the train started moving again, everyone grew quiet, each of us lost in our own thoughts. We couldn't imagine what sort of lives awaited us. We wondered whether we would ever be reunited with the families we'd left behind. A year and a half later, I would join my parents and brother in America; others would lose their parents and siblings to the gas chambers or bullets.

At last, we pulled into Victoria Station and I got off the train. London stretched out before me, gray and chill and strange. Men in striped trousers and bowler hats carrying black umbrellas and folded newspapers under their arms strolled the city streets. Not a pair of lederhosen or Tyrolean leather shorts or a single feathered Tyrolean hat was to be seen. I walked, not knowing where, carrying my heavy suitcase. The people looked taller than in Austria, with a variety of skin tones I had seen only in books and movies. The people seemed reserved, minding their own business.

Dusty and grimy, I needed a bath. I also needed directions to the street where I was supposed to find the woman who was my father's distant relative. Most of all, I needed a meal. I saw no coffee houses, no confection shops displaying Linzer tortes, Sacher tortes, or tiered, cream-filled mocha cakes.

I wandered into a crowded, smoke-filled restaurant unlike any I had ever seen. It was a pub, where men were drinking ale, eating, talking, laughing, and—strangest of all to me—playing darts. They looked a little curiously at me but not unkindly. By then, England was becoming accustomed to refugees.

I sat down at an empty table, and soon a tall, thin waiter with a worn face approached me with a menu. I stared at it and shook my head, indicating I couldn't understand it. He looked thoughtful, then pointed to various dishes people were eating at neighboring tables. The food all looked strange to me, until I spotted something that resembled knockwurst—two large sausages and a mound of something covered with brown gravy. I pointed to it.

"Bangers and mash," the waiter said, nodding as he jotted it on his pad.

The sausages weren't at all like knockwurst, and the mashed potatoes were very different from the boiled potatoes I was accustomed to. But I ate ravenously. When I finished my meal, the waiter brought my check. Not only did I not understand how much I owed, but I suddenly remembered to my horror that I had no money. I didn't know how to convey this in words, so I put my hands in both of my pockets, removed them, and held out my empty palms. I had never felt so mortified in my life. What would I do? What would they do to me? I wanted to run away.

"*Wer wird dafür zhalen?*" I asked in a faltering voice. Who will pay for it?

An elderly man, who had observed the scene and overheard me, approached the waiter and whispered a translation in his ear. The waiter looked at me—at my distraught expression, my heavy suitcase, my wrinkled clothes.

Sixty-two years later I still remember the eloquence of his gesture as he raised his eyes and pointed upward.

"God," he murmured.

~*Bluma Schwarz, as told by her husband*

Not Alone

The boy with the long, shaggy hair leaned against the wall, coolly watching me as I started class. He knew his assigned seat. He just hadn't decided yet whether he was willing to let me be in charge.

Peggy put her squeeze bottle of purple juice in the center of her table and sat staring at me as she toyed with the earring looped through her nose. Aware that our school doesn't permit eating or drinking in class, she resembled a fox lying in wait for my reaction.

As I was eyeing those two and contemplating my response, a new student walked into my already crowded room and handed me his pass. Wearing elbow-length, black rubber gloves with the fingertips cut out, he used those freed fingers to push his stringy blond hair out of his eyes. He whispered, "I got kicked out of my English class last semester.

Mrs. Harding said she thought I'd like this class better."

Thanks a lot, Susan! I thought; the student's case manager was a good friend of mine. *It looks like you sent me a winner this time.*

Turning my back to the class, I quickly wrote a word puzzle on the board. A rubber band whizzed over my head and hit the blackboard. Now, I was fighting down anger. Swallowing my desire to scream, I turned to face my class; it took only seconds to identify the culprit.

"Jim, go down to the office. The rest of you, get to work. Play time is over."

I had been teaching for many years, and each year the job got more difficult. I found myself wondering why I stuck with it.

As the students became engrossed in solving the puzzle, I quietly dealt with my problem students one at a time until my classroom was calm and under control. Then we began our lesson for the day. It was the third day of the new semester, and I was already tired and discouraged.

After classes ended for the day, I dragged myself into the principal's office and threw myself into her only chair. Janet, my principal, is also an old friend, but she barely looked up from her paperwork as I complained about my large classes and my overload of difficult students. When I finally finished my grumbling monologue and fell silent, she looked up.

"All English classes have at least thirty-five kids; you know that," she said evenly. "You have more difficult kids than most teachers because you're good with them. That's just the way it is. Those kids need you."

She returned to the work on her desk. I knew I had been dismissed.

Returning to my classroom, I picked up a book and slammed it against my desk as hard as I could. Bitterly, I addressed the empty room.

"The more successful I am with my students, the more problem kids they assign me. What a reward!"

I didn't have the energy to cry.

I was quiet at home that night; I didn't want to take out my anger and frustration on my own kids. When the four of them were all either sleeping or doing homework, I sat quietly in my bedroom and tried to think. I was ashamed at my resentment, but it was pushing deeper inside of me.

"Dear God," I prayed. "I don't want to do this job anymore. If you want me to continue, please let me know." It was a weak prayer, but it was all I could muster.

The phone rang, and I answered it reluctantly.

"Mrs. Zywicki?" The voice was vaguely familiar. "This is Pete Johnson. I just called to say thank you for everything you did for me last year. I'm sorry I gave you such a bad time in class. My dad had just gone to prison, and I was miserable. You helped me a lot, even though I didn't show it. I just wanted you to know."

"Thanks, Pete," I almost shouted. "You've made my day; you've really made my day."

"And thank you, God, for reminding me you are with me," I whispered as I placed the phone in the cradle.

Pete's call came six years ago, and I'm still teaching. In fact, the class I was so frustrated with at the time turned out to be one of my favorites. My faith in my students and myself continued to grow that semester, as it has with each year and each class since. My job isn't so hard when I remember what I'm working for and that I'm not working alone.

~Lou Killian Zywicki

Gratitude Harvest

I needed new walking shoes. That's how it all started. I had moved far from home to take a new job, and I still didn't have enough vacation days to return for Thanksgiving. I thought that if I spent a lot of time outside walking, it might make me feel less lonely and depressed.

There was a run-down shopping center near my place of employment with a discount shoe store—in addition to a no-name grocery store, a dollar store, one of those places that cashes checks, and a pet shop. I went there after work on the Wednesday before Thanksgiving. The day was cold and gray, and I was feeling three shades of blue. I had nothing but time to kill before I trudged back home to my empty, one-bedroom apartment, so I walked over to the grocery store for a hot cup of coffee to cheer myself up.

"How ya doing, brother?" came a booming voice as I approached the store. A huge black man in a too-tight coat embraced my hand in a grip that could easily have swallowed me up to my elbows.

"No sir, I'm not selling a single solitary thing," he insisted. "I'm just spreading the good word about Harvest House, a simple little place that I and nine other down-on-our-luck gentlemen like to call home."

As he let go of my hand, I felt a thin, folded pamphlet remain in my palm.

"Would you care to make a donation and help our holiday be a little more thankful?" he asked.

I looked up at his warm green eyes and broad bright smile. Something about his gentle, if booming, voice kindled something deep inside me. His weathered coat made me appreciate the life I led.

Figuring I had enough change in my pocket for the coffee and could always charge the shoes and a couple of pizzas over the long weekend ahead, I pulled out my wallet and gave him what little money I had. His eyes lit up as I dropped two fives and a single dollar bill into a grimy plastic jar full of dull pennies and bright quarters.

"Now, that's what I'm talking about!" he shouted as he clapped me on the back and sent me sprawling into the warm grocery store. "Happy Thanksgiving, brother!"

As I waited for the listless teenager behind the deli counter to brew up a fresh pot of "gourmet" coffee, I perused the cheaply printed Harvest House brochure, which spoke of "casting a net out into the sea of doomed lives and reeling in lost souls." The brochure's cover showed a picture of Harvest House. It looked barely big enough to hold the gentle giant outside, let alone nine other weary, downtrodden men.

I read of the morning scripture classes those men attended, of their daily work program, and of their practice of pooling the money they made for such necessities as toothpaste and milk. Their curfew was 8:00 P.M., and lights-out was at 11:00, every night.

I don't know why that flimsy little brochure calmed me so, but I found it strangely comforting. The idea of a safe bed in which to sleep, a cup of coffee and a comforting Bible passage to start the day, honest work, and a roof over one's head all seemed so simple. By the time I had paid for my steaming cup of vanilla mocha java, I felt so warm inside I didn't need it anymore.

"Now, this is too much!" shouted the friendly giant as I handed him the steaming Styrofoam cup. "I can't accept this!" he said as his eyes searched mine, confirming my simple offer.

Sneaking a peek back at him from a few steps away, I saw him take his first tentative sip.

Christmas carols were playing in the shoe store, where I found a stack of decent walking shoes marked for clearance at $9.99. I tried on a pair in my size and looked at their ridiculous blue racing stripes in the ankle-high mirror bolted to the floor. But how comfortable they were. How firm and solid on my tired feet.

Then I thought, "If they feel like that to me, how much more comforting and welcome would they feel on a pair of worn feet starting a new life?" Saying a short, silent prayer that my credit-card company had processed my last payment, I made a quick estimate of the shoe size of the mountainous man outside the grocery store.

"Excuse me," I asked the cashier, "Do you have these in a size fourteen, extra wide?"

I had just enough quarters in my car ashtray for a drive-through Thanksgiving Eve dinner at Taco Bell. As I drove to the address on the Harvest House brochure my stomach rumbled from the fast-food smells emanating from the backseat, where my dinner waited among the towering boxes of ten brand-new pairs of shoes.

Along the way I stopped at a dimly lit gas station to use the restroom and ask for directions. I patiently waited as the elderly man behind the counter spent nearly ten minutes recounting the history of the street

I was on and another ten minutes drawing me a map that resembled Bluebeard's guide to lost treasure.

By the time I got back to my car, it was so dark outside I didn't notice the shattered glass of my rear window until the broken glass crunched beneath the soles of my new shoes. It didn't take long, however, to realize that whoever had so stealthily broken it had also taken every pair of shoes I'd bought with my newly maxed-out credit card. The thief had even stolen my spicy soft tacos!

I thought of just turning around and heading home, but somehow that just didn't seem like an option. I thought about the men at Harvest House with their ratty old shoes and peaceful evening Bible readings and wondered what to tell them when I finally got there. I needn't have worried.

"Well, there he is!" boomed the mountainous man who, thankfully, remembered me from earlier in the afternoon when I knocked on their flimsy front door. "Mr. Big Spender. What a nice surprise. And just in time for dinner."

Before I could explain my miserable failure, his oak-solid arm whisked me into a warm, inviting dining room full of smiling faces and hands clasped in preparation for saying grace.

"We've got a visitor," the big man said, as the room full of men waited for me to speak.

But I couldn't. I grunted something that might have sounded like "shoes," but it was quickly lost in the silent stream of tears leaking from my tired eyes. What could I say about their shoes, about what I thought they might have meant to them? How could I tell them it would be another month before I could save up the money to replace them? How could I admit that I didn't even have enough money for dinner that night or anyone to share it with?

In moments, ten pairs of gentle arms surrounded me. They patted my back and said reassuring things like, "We know, man," and "We've all been there, son." I sniffled and snuffed and tried to explain, but they wouldn't have any of it.

Instead, they welcomed me to their table as if they'd been expecting me. There was only one catch.

"The new guy," said the mountainous man, "has to say grace."

"Dear God," I began softly as I tried to conceal my new shoes beneath their humble table, "thank you for the food we are about to eat and for the new friends I am about to share it with."

~Rusty Fischer

A Softer Heart

Miserable. I was just plain miserable. We'd moved from our farm in Oklahoma to the gritty Gulf Coast town of Galveston, Texas, and I was none too happy about it. Papa worked as a stevedore foreman on the Galveston wharves. He'd initially gone there to help with the war effort, but after the war he'd stayed on to save money to buy more land in Oklahoma.

I had just entered my teens, and I was moody, rebellious, and angry at being dragged off to Texas. I'd loved our two-room school back home and hated the school in Galveston. I missed my grandparents and my friends in Oklahoma, and our dingy, crowded apartment in Galveston couldn't hold a candle to the freedom and homey comfort of our farm.

I knew my parents were worried about me, their firstborn. But they knew nothing about adolescent rebellion. They'd both grown up in large, impoverished families on poor little cotton farms, where they'd worked so hard to help keep food on the table, they'd had no time or energy to rebel against stern parents. Besides, sassing and disobeying would not have been allowed or tolerated.

I knew all that, but I didn't much care. It was a miserable time for me, and I retaliated by making my parents as miserable as I could. Finally, my exasperated mother turned me over to my father and instructed him to "give the girl a good bawling out." The thing was, Papa was a conflict avoider, especially with me. He usually left the "fussing and spanking" to Mama, but she had thrown the ball into his court and dealing with me had become his responsibility. Papa's strategy was to take me out to the movies, thinking he'd slip in his lecture sometime during the evening. Of course, I was on to him.

We started out by going to see a rip-roaring western. Papa and I both loved westerns, so while we watched the movie in the darkened theater, it was easy to forget our problems. When the lights went up, we reluctantly came back to the present. He visibly began to brace himself for the "talking-to" he had to deliver, while I stiffened in anticipation.

Papa took me to the Star Dairy. Over chocolate malts, he tried to set me straight, but he never quite pulled it off. After several false starts, we just sat and savored our malts in silence. I tried to keep my eyes on the slowly shrinking contents of my malt glass, but every so often, I'd steal a glance at Papa. I noticed how much he'd aged since we left the farm; he seemed older than his forty-four years. New furrows creased his brow; deep lines ran from his nose to his chin; and his hands were gnarled and toil worn. Grueling sixteen-hour days on the waterfront had taken their toll—and so, most likely, had a rebellious daughter, I suddenly realized.

"*Oh no you don't,*" I thought, banishing my unwanted thoughts of compassion. I was still young, even if my parents weren't, and I had my own life to live. I hardened my heart and tried not to notice my father's worried glances in my direction. We drove home in silence. Later I heard him quietly assure my mother that everything would be okay.

The next morning Papa dropped me off at school on his way to work. He told me I'd have to take the bus or walk home after school, because he was going to pick up some gear on the Galveston waterfront and then drive over to Texas City to supervise the loading of the *High Flyer*. I'll never forget the look of shock and happiness on his face when I impulsively leaned over and kissed him goodbye. I had not voluntarily kissed either of my parents in a long while.

Later that morning, as I labored over my sketch of the alimentary canal in science class, my pencil suddenly wobbled crazily out of my hand, across the page, and off the desk. A tremor had shaken the whole building and a strange sound pulsed in our ears. Everyone in the classroom turned to look out the north windows and saw a terrifying mushroom cloud rising in the blue April sky. Although, in 1947, we were still very new to the atomic age, we knew about mushroom clouds. A huge crack had spread across the library wall upstairs, sending teachers and students screaming down the hall. Pale-faced, our young science teacher quickly organized us as if for a fire drill. She had to stop and assist Lonnie James and Luther Hill, who had both wedged themselves under the same desk and were stuck fast.

We huddled in little groups on the beach side of the school grounds and watched the spreading cloud darken the bright spring sky. The falling embers soon blackened my new lavender cotton dress. Everyone was abuzz, wondering what in the world had happened. Rumors flew every which way, although two hours would pass before we got the full story. One rumor we heard was that the Texas City Monsanto Chemical plant had blown up; children whose parents worked there began to weep. I was trying to comfort one of them when someone else said that ammonium nitrate had exploded on the *Grand Camp*, destroying that ship as well as the *High Flyer* berthed alongside it.

I froze—that was where my father was working that day. The playground and fields seemed to recede from my vision, and I felt as if I were floating somewhere beyond it all, observing the others and myself as if from another dimension. In my mind's eye, I saw Papa sitting hunched and worried, haggard and old-looking, at the drugstore counter the night before. Proud like the rest of our Scotch-Irish-Cherokee clan, I wasn't about to let anyone see me cry, so I wandered off to a far corner of the schoolyard. As the ocean spray from the gulf streaked the black smudges on my dress, face, and hair, I counted sea gulls and looked for four-leaf clovers, fighting back the tears and silently praying, "Please, Lord, not Papa, not my papa."

The dark cloud from Texas City soon blotted out the sunlight, while cinders continued to rain down on us as we shivered in the chilly air. Luther Hill came over and sat down beside me. We had been friends since the seventh grade, friendly competitors for the best grades in math and riding the same bus to and from school. Luther was short, freckle-faced, a little overweight, and totally lacking in athletic prowess. Some of the other boys teased him unmercifully, but he took it with good humor and grace. If I'd had a brother, I would have wanted one like Luther Hill.

"Kathryn Jane, where is your dad working today?" he asked, the top of his freckled nose crinkling with concern.

"He had to pick up some things at Pier 29. Then he was going to work on the *High Flyer.*" My voice wavered on the ship's name.

I looked more closely at Luther. His face was wan. I didn't have to ask him where his father was; Luther talked all the time about his dad's job at Monsanto Chemical.

The school bell summoned us back inside, and we were dismissed to find our way home the best way we could. There were no buses, because they were all being used to help evacuate the living and the dead from Texas City. I'd walked a quarter of the three-mile trip to my home when a car horn startled me to attention. My Uncle Barney pulled up alongside me in his old Ford. The instant I saw him, I knew my father was gone. Otherwise, Papa would have come for me himself.

As if in slow motion from a great distance, Uncle Barney motioned for me to get in. Numb with grief, I crawled into the back seat. I barely took notice of the man sitting there, didn't recognize him until he reached for me. When Papa put his strong arms around me, I forgot for a moment that Scotch-Irish Cherokees aren't supposed to cry.

We listened to Papa tell the story of his "deliverance" over and over again. It was the first time in his long working life that he had ever been late to a job. He'd lost his warehouse keys and had been crawling around on the Galveston docks looking for them when the ships exploded across the bay. If not for his keys slipping through that hole in his pocket, he almost certainly would have gone up with the *High Flyer*. We later learned that the blast had obliterated the two ships and four square miles of Texas City and that more than 600 people were dead or missing.

It took us more than an hour to cross the main intersection in Galveston on our drive home that day. We watched a continuous parade of buses, trucks, ambulances, and cars carrying victims to the two hospitals. World War II was still a vivid memory at the time, and I remember thinking, "This must be what war-ravaged countries are like." I also remember feeling a powerful barrage of emotions surge through me as I experienced my first transcendent moment. I felt thankful to live in a war-free country. I felt grief for the victims and their families. I felt luminous joy that my father's life had been spared. And I wondered at the great mysteries of life and death.

Many of my fellow students lost their parents in the explosion; Luther Hill's father disappeared without a trace. Tragedy would one day come to our family, as it inevitably comes to all, but on the day Texas City blew up, it miraculously passed us by. Because he lost his keys on that April morning, my father lived for another thirty-two years and I found my way again.

~Kathryn Thompson Presley

A Gift from
Christmas Angels

I usually made myself crazy with the holidays and had vowed to simplify that year. I had done my best to stick to my promise, and by the Saturday two weeks before Christmas, I felt that I really had a handle on my holiday preparations. Gifts had been bought and wrapped, menus had been planned, and the tree was up and decorated. Packages for faraway friends and relations were ready for Monday's mail, and the presents that would travel north with me to my hometown later that week had been wrapped, tagged, and stacked on the kitchen counter. I planned to drive "home" to Bangor, Maine, later that week for my traditional just-before-Christmas visit.

The highlight of that day trip would be having a good long tête-à-tête with my grandmother, whom I adored. We'd munch Christmas cookies and sip tea as we caught up and reminisced and laughed. There would be much laughter. Later that afternoon, I would make my rounds to other relatives, delivering gifts and glad tidings of the season. With the numerous visits and six-hour round trip, it would be an exhausting day, but one I made willingly. The chance to spend the day with my grandmother, my truest friend, was reason enough. Though we talked on the phone at least once a week, I treasured every moment of her company.

With my Christmas tasks well in hand, I decided to tackle the three-foot-high pile of ironing that sat before me. Christmas carols blaring from the stereo and the aroma of hand-dipped chocolates drying on the counter made for a merry atmosphere, despite the mundane task at hand.

"I need to go to Bangor," I suddenly said, iron midair, to my husband.

"Uh-huh. On Thursday, right?"

"No, today. I think I should go today," I found myself answering.

"Today?" he asked, putting down the newspaper and looking at me over the rims of his glasses.

"Yes, as soon as I finish the ironing and a few other little chores."

"But the day is already half over. When were you planning to leave?"

"Actually, I hadn't planned it, but I should be able to leave by eight o'clock."

"Tonight?" he asked again. Not one to question my judgment, he paused to consider what was clearly an unusually impulsive decision on my part. "I'd really rather you not drive all that way alone at night."

"I suppose you're right."

I continued to make my way through the ironing, stopping only to answer the phone and to brew a fresh pot of coffee. As I ironed, I made a mental list of the few remaining things to do before Christmas, but the urge to drop everything and go to Bangor nagged at the back of my mind.

When I finally reached the bottom of the pile, my friend Colleen joined me for coffee. Colleen has lived with us for years. As she didn't have much family of her own, we had adopted her into ours. My kids call her Auntie. I told her about wanting to drive to Bangor that night and my husband's concern.

"I could go with you," she volunteered.

My husband, overhearing our conversation, piped in, "If Auntie goes with you, go for it. My only concern was you driving alone at night."

We decided to drive straight through and get a hotel room in Bangor. I hated imposing on relatives that late, and I loved hotels. It would make our ladies' night out a little more fun. By 7:30, we were loading overnight bags, gifts, and homemade goodies into the back of my station wagon. Armed with the cell phone, a thermos of coffee, Christmas CDs, snacks for the drive, and kisses and hugs from my husband and children, we left on our three-hour journey.

A few minutes later, the first snow flurry of the season began, covering the pavement with a pretty white dusting and adding to the feeling of festivity. But with each mile, the snow fell harder. Within minutes, several inches of icy snow had accumulated on the highway. My rear-wheel-drive car didn't do well in slippery conditions, so I slowed to 45 miles per hour. The wind began to kick up and the snow started falling in sheets, reducing my visibility to the short range directly ahead of my headlight beams. I slowed to 25 miles per hour and followed the white reflective markers along the right side of the highway, struggling to keep the car on the road but remaining strangely calm. Something inside told me we'd be okay.

Without warning, the white markers and then the pavement suddenly disappeared. As we plowed into a thick layer of untouched snow, the car's rear wheels lost traction and we started to fishtail. Somehow I was able to regain control before we hit the snowdrift alongside the road.

"You're off the highway!" Colleen cried out.

Though rattled, I quickly collected myself. I realized I'd followed the highway markers off of an exit ramp. We were in the middle of nowhere in the pitch dark, and the snow was deep. I turned the car around, praying we wouldn't get stuck, and we found our way back to the highway.

For another 100 miles, we crept through the blizzard. The snowstorm finally let up about thirty minutes south of Bangor. By then, we were laughing about our ordeal and preparing to enjoy our evening. We reached our exit safely and looked for a motel. A country inn near the exit had always intrigued me, but I'd never stayed there. Most overnights in Bangor included my children and required larger accommodations. We decided to give it a try.

To our delight, the inn was beautifully adorned for Christmas. Our room was decorated in a country motif, and a large Christmas wreath hung outside the window. With the gently falling snow as a backdrop, it looked like a scene from an old-fashioned Christmas card, which is what I told my husband when I phoned him to announce our safe, if somewhat delayed, arrival. Colleen and I spent the night talking, giggling, and watching television. It was one o'clock before we fell asleep.

In the morning I called my aunt to ask what time would be convenient to visit Gram.

"She was having trouble breathing this morning, so they took her to the hospital," my aunt said.

Though concerned, I was not unduly alarmed. My grandmother had a history of breathing difficulties, and the staff at the assisted-living facility where she now lived often took her to the hospital for nebulizer treatments to ease her congestion.

"I'll call you later to find out when to come up," I told my aunt.

Colleen and I spent the rest of the morning browsing through bookstores and sipping hot cider. After lunch, I called my aunt back.

"The doctor decided to admit her," she said. "By the time you get there, she'll be settled into her room."

Minutes later we arrived at the hospital and took the elevator to the geriatric ward. Gram was sitting in a wheelchair while a nurse got her ready for bed. Her breathing was labored, and it was difficult for her to speak, so I translated. I understood what she was trying to say. She pointed to her cheek, signaling Colleen to plant a kiss there. She gestured that her feet were cold, and the nurse brought her socks. When she ran her fingers over my shiny, polished nails, she was telling me she needed a manicure.

"We'll get Karen over here tomorrow to do your nails," I told her. My sister often did Gram's nails when she visited.

The afternoon passed quickly and pleasantly. Gram dozed from time to time, but for most of the visit, she was alert and animated. She smiled often as we chatted, and she held my hand tightly.

At the end of our visit, I wished her a Merry Christmas. I whispered that her Christmas presents were at my aunt's house and that she'd better behave and not open them until Christmas.

"You're the best Christmas present," she told me. She said it every year.

She reached for me, and when I leaned down, she hugged me fiercely and kissed my cheek. I kissed her forehead and told her I loved her. She smiled and nodded, unable to gather enough breath to speak.

From the doorway I heard her strained, "I love you."

I turned back and smiled, our eyes meeting.

The trip home was uneventful. We arrived mid-evening to warm greetings from the family. After conveying my concerns about Gram to my husband, I called my aunt to say we'd arrived home safely. She'd just returned from the hospital after having tucked Gram in for the night.

"I told her I'd see her in the morning," she said. "And she blew me a kiss."

Gram died an hour later.

When the call came, I felt overwhelming grief—but also gratitude for the privilege of being able to spend one last peaceful, enjoyable afternoon with her.

During the two weeks before her death, Gram had seen almost everyone in the family who lived within a reasonable driving distance. Although we often spoke on the phone, I hadn't seen her in two months, and I knew how much she cherished our time together. I also know now that the strength with which she held my hand was her sign to me that she was strong in spirit and that she was saying goodbye.

In the eulogy I delivered at Gram's funeral, I talked about her love and devotion to her family. I spoke of her strength and courage, which had enabled her to raise six children alone after having been widowed in her forties. I said that, rather than mourning our loss, we should celebrate with gratitude the many years she had graced our lives. And I talked about angels.

How else could I explain my compulsion to drive three hours at night to see her, days before my planned trip? Or being guided through a blinding snowstorm? Or the miraculous gift of those last precious hours with her?

I had been blessed with the love and friendship of an angel here on earth—my grandmother. Angels had brought me to Gram for a final Christmas visit. Now she dwells with them, in comfort and joy.

~Kimberly Ripley

A Stranger in the House

When I woke up the other morning, I found a stranger in my house. You could say he bears a slight resemblance to my oldest son, but not much, because my son is just a little boy.

"Who are you?" I asked the towering stranger, trying to stare him down—although my direct line of sight only reached his Adam's apple. I looked up to his face and noticed eight unmistakable mustache hairs.

"Aww, Mom!" The stranger seemed to know me. For an instant I would have bet he was about to pat my head. Instead, he handed me a cup of coffee, which he'd made himself, then crossed the kitchen in three broad, determined steps on feet that appeared to be at least the size of those of a Sasquatch.

Unlike this stranger, my little boy can't leave the

kitchen without running around the table in mad

circles just for the heck of it, sometimes trailing a toy on a string, enjoying the sound of his feetie pajamas scooching over the tiles.

A bit later I heard the stranger in the shower, warbling about living *la vida loca*.

My little boy doesn't live *la vida loca*. He lives *la vida* Legos. He spends his entire day stacking block after block into identical towering rectangles, which he later informs me are dinosaurs, airplanes, buildings, or robots—rolling his eyes in disbelief that I'm unable to see what's plainly in front of my face.

The stranger came out of the shower, and a fog of hair-product, deodorant, and cologne fumes rolled out after him. My little boy smells like peanut butter and Play-Doh.

The stranger stopped to check his image in a mirror, and unable to find an errant hair escaping his moussed locks, he lumbered off, satisfied. My little boy has a wild cowlick in the back of his head, which he refuses to let anyone near.

The stranger was now doing something in my laundry room. Curious, I followed. He opened the dryer, removed some shirts, and put them on hangers.

"You have to take them out right away, so they don't wrinkle," he informed me in a voice that started out bass but crackled back to alto.

My little boy's understanding of the dryer is limited to how loud his voice sounds if he sticks his head inside and bellows, "I am the master of this cave!" Or how loud his mother's voice sounds when she hollers, "Who left these crayons in his pants pocket?"

"I can't wear a wrinkled shirt to school, you know," the stranger continued. My little boy wears his favorite Batman shirt for three weeks solid. I have to sneak it off of him at night to wash it, and then return it before he wakes up.

I gathered the stranger was now hungry, as I saw him toast a loaf of bread and crack a dozen eggs. You have to wrestle my little boy away from cartoons in the morning to get him to eat half a bowl of cereal.

The stranger said it was time for him to get to school and he gathered his things. I asked him what grade he was in.

"Geez, Mom, seventh. I started junior high this week. What's wrong with you?" he asked.

Then he bent down to kiss me on the cheek. My little boy runs up to me and hugs my leg, staring way up at me, and smiling his goofy, mom-adoring smile.

I followed the stranger out the door, pausing in the driveway to watch him stride to the corner, where he waited for his bus with girls who have breasts. My little boy goes to kindergarten with girls who have pigtails. The stranger didn't so much as glance toward the house when the bus came. My little boy always runs for one last hug before he goes through the kindergarten door. He is never the first to let go.

Later, the stranger returned to my house, apparently believing he lives here. After consuming half the contents of the refrigerator, he claimed his father left him instructions the night before to teach my oldest daughter (who I swear is just a toddler) how to cut the grass.

I joined the stranger out on the lawn and watched as he showed his younger sibling the mechanics of the mower, patiently and carefully detailing safety instructions.

"Are you listening to me, or do you just want to fool around?" he asks my daughter, who has been busy rolling her eyes. "I'm not talking for my health, you know."

He showed her how to turn corners, empty the catcher, fill the mower with gas, and pull the cord to start the beast. He demonstrated the "proper" row, unable to resist showing off by pushing the mower with one hand before turning it, like a runner's baton, over to his sister.

In an instant, she was off cutting her own paths, not exactly the same way he had done it, but capably.

The stranger turned to me and said, "She's doing better than I expected. She's actually doing a good job. It's funny how fast they grow up, huh?" He elbowed me in the ribs and laughed.

I stared at the stranger—who, now that I think of it, will always look exactly like my little boy—and smiled.

~Denise Wahl

The Walk of Courage

The school day was over. The halls that had bustled with activity just a few minutes earlier were now quiet. As I waited near the entryway by the big double door, one of my classmates came to stand beside me. Her mouth popped open in surprise and her eyes grew round as she stared through the window.

"What's wrong with her?" she whispered.

Out on the sidewalk, my mother made her way toward the building, moving one crutch at a time and then carefully swinging each leg forward. Every half dozen steps or so, she stopped to get a better grip on the handle of her purse. It took her many long minutes to walk the short distance from the curb to the door.

Mom had scheduled a parent-teacher conference for right after school. All the previous conferences had taken place later in the afternoon, and by the time my mom had come to the school, I was already on the school bus, heading home to our Wisconsin farm. This would be my first opportunity to show her my classroom. It would also be the first opportunity for some of my schoolmates—those who were waiting for rides or had after-school activities—to see my mother.

Right after the buses left, I had seen Dad drive up and let Mom out of the car in front of the school. I knew she'd need my help getting through the double doors, so I had made sure I was already waiting.

My classmate repeated her question more insistently. "What happened to her?"

I thought for a few moments, wondering how best to explain it. Finally I decided to take the most direct route.

"She had polio," I said.

"Oh."

She watched my mother for a few seconds longer. "When will she get better?"

"She won't."

My friend remained quiet for several more moments. "What is polio, anyway?" she finally asked—another question for which I felt I didn't have a good answer.

"Well, first you get really sick, like you have the flu," I said. "And then you can't walk."

My friend turned quickly in my direction, her eyes wide with alarm. "Like the flu? Can we catch it?"

"Oh no," I hastily assured her. "The polio happened a long time ago. Before I was born. That's why we get polio shots, to keep us from getting it."

My classmate turned toward the door again to watch my mother's approach. "But why didn't your mom get any better?"

My mother had contracted polio in 1942, when she had been twenty-six years old and my brother and sister had been five and three years old. I was born sixteen years later, long after the doctors had told her she'd never have more children. From an early age, I'd known all about my mother's condition. I realized, however, that my classmate might have trouble understanding that Mom was as "better" as she'd ever be. I tried to explain anyway.

"Well, she did get better," I said. "When she had polio, she was really, really sick. She was in the hospital for six months."

"Six months?" my friend echoed.

"Then she got better and came home," I added. "But even though she wasn't sick anymore, the polio made it so she could never walk well again."

My mother had gone into the hospital, 250 miles from our home, in November and had not been released until May. That meant that she had missed her birthday and Christmas with her family, as well as her wedding anniversary and the birthdays of both my brother and sister. During the course of her illness, the polio had partially paralyzed her right leg and had completely paralyzed her left leg.

Mom finally reached the big double doors. I went out and held the outer door open for her. After she passed through the first door, my classmate held open the second one.

"Hi, Mrs. Ralph," she said, smiling shyly.

My mother returned her smile. "Thank you very much for holding the door. That's a big help to me."

The three of us walked slowly toward the classroom.

"Does it hurt?" my friend blurted. "The polio, I mean."

"No," Mom said, moving one crutch and then one leg forward. "It doesn't hurt. I just can't walk very fast, that's all."

"I'm glad," my friend said. "I mean, I'm glad it doesn't hurt."

My mother smiled again at the girl.

As my mother entered my classroom, I overheard someone else ask, "What's wrong with her?"

I cringed, feeling embarrassed that other kids were talking about my mother in her presence.

"She had polio," I heard my friend reply.

"Oh. What is polio, anyway?"

Mom caught my eye. "It's okay," she said quietly. "They're just curious."

My teacher rose from behind her desk to greet my mother, and I left the room to go see if my dad had parked the car and might be waiting by the office. In the hall, a boy who was a few years older than I was asked, "Did your mom really have polio?"

"Yeah, she did."

"I kinda thought maybe that other girl was making it up," he explained. "So now your mom has to walk really slow?"

"That's right."

"I hope she gets better," he said before hurrying away.

I didn't bother trying to explain to him that Mom wouldn't get any "better."

In the following years, my mother's visits to school for conferences or special programs continued to draw stares and whispers. But as more children got to know her, more kids held the door for her and said kind hellos. Mom always made sure to politely return their greeting, smile, and thank them for their help. The kids would usually smile shyly in return; some would say, "You're welcome," as we'd been taught by our parents and teachers.

Early on I had become my mother's helper, performing those tasks that were beyond her capabilities: shaking a rug, getting the mail, or running to answer the telephone. Helping my mother was second nature to me. I'd never thought much about how devastating the effects of polio must have been for her. After all, when you grow up in a situation like that, it seems "normal" to you.

It wasn't until I started to see my mother through other people's eyes—like those of the kids at school—that I began to recognize her courage and the dignity with which she walked through life, moving one crutch, and then one leg, forward at a time.

~LeAnn R. Ralph

Monsters of the Sky

My four-year-old nephew Max had golden brown hair tinged with a hint of strawberry and enormous brown eyes that touched something deep inside me. But behind those beautiful eyes was a boy who was terrified of thunderstorms.

When lightning streaked the sky and thunder rumbled, Max's eyes would grow wide and deep, as if holding a well of fear. One day while I was visiting Max and his family, a flash of lightning tore the sky in two with a jagged line that seemed to connect heaven and earth. The thunder that followed seemed to raise Max a few inches off the ground. He looked like a little tin soldier—his arms folded tightly over his chest, his body stiff. He paced the room, repeating, "I'm scared! I'm scared!"

As I watched him walk nervously back and forth, I searched my mind for something that might calm him. Remembering that when I was young, my mother had told me that thunder was the noise angels made when they bowled, I repeated the story to Max. It failed to ease his discomfort. Then I remembered how, when my children had been his age, I used to have them draw the things that frightened them.

I said, "Max, let's go sit down and draw the lightning!"

He quickly reminded me, "I'm scared of lightning!"

"Yes, I can see how afraid you are," I said. "Come with me and we'll draw that scary sky together."

Max looked up at me tentatively, curious about this aunt who wanted to draw lightning. While his family waited out the storm before the TV, Max and I went into the kitchen and found a place to draw the frightening behavior of the sky.

Max slowly climbed up on the black-and-white metal stool at the kitchen counter while I found some drawing tools in my sister's kitchen. I placed a dull pencil and some scraps of white paper in front of him.

In a near whisper, Max confided, "I don't know how to draw lightning."

"Would you like me to draw some first?"

"Yes," he answered, briefly distracted from his

fear. His eyes grew round with curiosity as I quickly sketched a few jagged lines.

"There," I said, smiling. "Do you want to take a turn now?"

Max cautiously took the pencil and drew one small saw-tooth line. He looked up at me for approval.

"Cool, Max! Wanna make another?" I said, handing him more paper.

He made more lightning bolts, each one a little larger and bolder than the last. As Max experimented with zigs and zags, he said, "There, that's a giant monster of the sky! This one's gonna be bigger!"

As he poured his terror onto the paper, his voice returned to normal, but his eyes continued to enlarge with fear whenever a thunderclap boomed.

"Where do you feel scared in your body, Max?" I asked.

"Here," he said, pointing to his chest.

"Put your hand where you feel it."

He put his hand over his heart. Then I placed one hand gently over his, while resting my other hand on his back. "Right here, huh?"

"Yeah."

I paused for a few moments. "How does it feel now?"

"A little better."

Max boldly drew a big, dark, jagged lightning streak.

"Are you afraid of lightning, Aunt Lou?"

"Yes, sometimes," I said softly, sensing that perhaps he needed some company in his fear.

Looking compassionately at me, his head tilted slightly to one side, Max reached over and put his hand just above my heart. "It hurts right here?" he asked.

Caught by surprise, I nodded. "Yes, sometimes a little."

The tenderness of my four-year-old nephew touched my soul and filled me with awe at how drawing monsters of the sky together could open both our hearts. That precious memory, created many years ago, sparked a connection between us that continues to this day.

~Louise Mathewson

Memoir of a Violin

I peered through the window of the charming little violin shop, and my heart began to race.

I'd been out with friends for my usual Friday evening of good food and good conversation. My dinner companions had decided to retire early, though, and since I wasn't ready to call it a night yet, I had decided to walk home from the restaurant rather than take a ride home with my friends. I'd traveled that way before, but I'd never noticed the quaint little shop or even the sign outside. Had I seen it, I probably would have hurried by or crossed the street to avoid it. But, for some reason, that night I felt drawn to the violin shop.

I wiped the condensation from the window with my jacket sleeve to get a better look inside. Several violins hung from the paint-chipped walls, patiently waiting to be repaired. As my eyes wandered around the room, I felt as though I were looking through a window into the past—my own past.

Once, many years before, the violin had been my passion.

As a child, I had attempted many pursuits, most of them chosen by my mother. "Join the swim team, Tara. Your sister, Monica, is a good swimmer; surely you will be, too." What my mother refused to acknowledge, however, was that I had an aversion to water. In fact, I was afraid of it—and still am today.

Every Saturday I begged my mother not to make me go to the swim meet, but she always prevailed. I would tremble with each bang of the starting pistol, and it would take every ounce of strength I had to dive into the cold water and swim to the other side of the pool as fast as I could. It was, of course, never fast enough. My arms would flap wildly and my feet kick recklessly while the other swimmers glided past me. I would have given it up long before I did if it had not been for my dad. From beneath the water I could hear the muffled sound of his encouraging shouts as he called my name and cheered me on. When at last I would raise my hand to grab the edge of the pool, he would always be there waiting for me with a warm, dry towel, telling me how proud he was of me for trying

Gymnastics was another sport my mother decided

would be good for me, partly because she'd been a gymnast when she was young. She didn't seem to consider the fact that I was extremely tall for my age and quite a few pounds overweight. To please her, I tried anyway. Much to my surprise and my mother's delight, I actually enjoyed my short-term fling in the world of pommel horses and parallel bars. I especially liked the trampoline. I spent most of my hour-long gymnastics class jumping as high as I could, trying to reach the asphalt ceiling.

My mother, however, wasn't satisfied with my simple mastery of bouncing up and down. I was strongly urged to attempt more daring feats of flexibility. In my effort to please her, however, I attempted more than I was capable of and ended up breaking my anklebone. The annoying limp I carry with me today is all that remains of my futile stint as a gymnast.

For most of my youth, I wondered if I would ever be good at anything. I certainly didn't have my mother's or my sister's athletic talents, nor did I have any interest in competitive sports—a fact my mother found difficult to understand. "Maybe I'm just not the athletic type," I would say. "Maybe you just don't try hard enough," she would respond.

My lack of an avocation was the subject of many disagreements between my parents. I'd lay awake at night, listening to them argue over my fate. "She needs to find something to do with herself and stick to it," Mom would say. "You need to let her discover her own talents and stop trying to make those decisions for her," Dad would argue. After one such argument, my father came into my room to say good night. When he kissed my cheek, his lips caught a fresh tear.

"Why are you crying, honey?" he asked.

"I just want to make her happy, Daddy," I said, choking on my tears. "I try and try, but nothing I do is ever good enough."

"That's not true, Tara," he said. "Your mother and I are so proud of you. . . ."

"No, she is not!"

"Of course she is," he said. "She just wants you to find the gifts God has blessed you with and use them wisely."

"What do you mean, gifts?"

"The special things that make you, you," he said. "If you look deep inside your heart, you'll find what it is that makes you shine."

"But how will I know what that is?"

"You'll know, honey. You'll know."

"But what if there isn't anything inside of me that shines?"

"Everyone shines, Tara," he said. "In their own way, everyone shines."

By junior high, I still hadn't found my way to shine.

One day our school's orchestra conductor and several of his protégés came into my classroom, where I'd been daydreaming as usual, and gave a demonstration. The drums annoyed me. The flutes bored me. But the violin. . . . Ah, the violin. It made the sweetest sound I'd ever heard. I seemed to rise and float on the silvery notes emanating from its delicately curved wooden body. I watched fascinated as the bow caressed the strings, imagining I was the one making this beautiful music. A warm glow enveloped me. For the first time in my life, I was enraptured and I was shining.

I ran all the way home after school, clutching the paperwork tightly. My hand trembled as I gave the permission slip to my parents, for I feared they might summarily dismiss my desire. They didn't. My mother was thrilled to see me finally excited about something, and my father winked at me as he eagerly signed the slip.

I took to the violin like a skylark to flight. In the small town where I grew up, few budding musicians chose to play the violin; in my case, it was as if the instrument had chosen me. I rose quickly in ability; before long I had landed the first seat in the community orchestra and had rated a feature story in the local newspaper. I'd found my calling and was on my way to a promising career as a professional violinist.

My family attended every concert I performed in, and their pride in me—especially my father's—was palpable. As soon as my bow hit the strings, his face would light up, and he was always the first to stand and applaud when I finished. Even my mother beamed, her eyes glistening, during my performances.

Every night after my father came home from his stressful job on the police force, he'd sit in his favorite chair with a beer in one hand and a cigarette in the other and listen to me practice. "Play me a song, Tara," he'd say. I was always happy to oblige. He would seem almost mesmerized by the music. That was the only time of the day I saw him totally relaxed.

One afternoon I came home from orchestra practice to find my sister wild-eyed and with tears streaming down her cheeks, frantically pressing the buttons on the phone.

"What's wrong?" I asked, terrified.

"Dad. Dad," was all she could say.

My hand still clutching my violin case, I ran to my parents' bedroom. My father was lying on the bed, and my mother was pounding on his chest.

"Daddy?" I called out to him. "Daddy? Daddy, what's the matter?"

"Get out, Tara! Get out now!" my mother commanded, furiously pumping his chest.

"But Mama, I—"

"Get out!" she bellowed, the sound of her voice scaring me almost as much as my motionless father.

I couldn't move—yet I couldn't just stand there doing nothing while the person I cherished above all others, my mentor and protector, died right before my eyes. I had to do something. There had to be something I could do to make him stay, to bring him back. People die; I understood that—but other people, not my dad. Fathers are supposed to live forever and never leave you.

As if in a trance, I hastily removed the violin from its case and began to play for my father. First Beethoven, then Orff; I played more fervently and passionately than I'd ever played before. I played and played, unable to stop—certain that if I did, my father would die. As the paramedics entered the bedroom and began working on my father, I continued playing. While they placed an oxygen mask over his mouth and electric paddles on his chest and tried reviving his lifeless body again and again, I played. I played so hard and fast I could have woken the dead. But I couldn't wake my father.

It wasn't until I heard the words, "I'm sorry, we did all we could," that I finally stopped playing and the beautiful music gave way to the horrified wails of my mother. I dropped the violin to the floor, vowing never to play again.

Staring at the woman reflected in the window of the violin shop, I barely recognized that young girl. It had been many years since I'd last thought of that harrowing afternoon, the memory of which I'd spent most of my life trying to repress. It had been even longer since I'd played the violin. True to my vow, I hadn't picked it up since my last solo performance for my father.

When I entered my apartment, I went directly to the closet and removed my violin from its case, where it had lain, untouched, for more than twenty years. With a soft cloth, I brushed the years of accumulated dust from its still lustrous wooden body, wondering if it could still be in tune. When I slid the bow across the strings, the violin made a low, rumbling sound, telling me it was not. I adjusted the knobs, surprised that I actually remembered how. I walked over to my dresser and stood before the picture of my father. I slowly raised the violin to my chin and held it securely to my shoulder. My hand quivered as I lifted the bow. I gingerly placed the rod on the strings, my trembling hand instantly calmed, and I began to play Pachelbel's Canon in D.

~*Theresa Marie Heim*

A Voice in the Storm

The little girl pressed her nose to the window and frowned at the storm outside. It was spring vacation in her small midwestern town, and it had been raining the entire week—ever since Easter Sunday. Her backyard was flooded, and a gray gloominess had descended on her house.

Nine-year-old Dolores loved playing outdoors and considered herself quite the adventurer. All morning, she kept returning to the window to glare at the dismal scene outside, willing the rain to stop. She would do anything—anything—to get out of that house.

Her escape came just before noon.

"Who wants to go to the store for me? We're all out of bread, and I thought we'd have soup and sandwiches for lunch," her mom asked, looking directly at Dolores's older brother, Warren. "The rain has slowed down, and if you carry my umbrella, you won't get wet." Warren stuck his nose deeper into his book and didn't say a word.

"I'll go!" Dolores chirped.

Her mother smiled. "I'll go get the umbrella and money. You put on your raincoat, honey."

Glad for an excuse to get out of the house, Dolores didn't mind the rain or that she was just running an errand. And she wasn't a bit afraid of going out in a storm—she was just walking to Canfield's, a small neighborhood delicatessen a couple of blocks away, after all.

Dolores skipped along the sidewalk. She rejoiced in the cool, fresh rain tickling her face and laughed as the wind tossed her hair all willy-nilly and played tug-of-war with the umbrella. She kicked and splashed through the puddles, just like Gene Kelly in *Singing in the Rain*. Dolores loved that movie.

She arrived at Canfield's within ten minutes. She went in and bought the loaf of bread, resisting the urge to buy penny candy, too. She didn't dawdle at all. But when she left the store, the sky suddenly darkened and the shower turned into a downpour. Bright bolts of lightning zigzagged across the sky, and angry bursts of thunder crashed around her. She clutched the umbrella tightly in one hand and tried to shield the bread from the cold rain with the other, as the wind tried to yank both away.

Anxious to get home and out of the storm, Dolores decided to take a shortcut through the grounds of the grammar school that she and her brothers attended. The school was a modern, three-story, red-brick building. Next to it stood the town's historic one-room schoolhouse, which was also made of red brick. Surrounding the school grounds was a heavy metal fence lined with a row of ancient elm trees.

Dolores cut across the schoolyard in front of the buildings and headed toward the gate in the fence leading to the sidewalk home. As she approached the gate, she looked up at the massive limbs of the elms, thrashing menacingly above her. Suddenly, just as she passed through the gate and under the trees, Dolores heard a voice calling her name and telling her to run. She stopped and looked back to see who it was, but no one was there. She shrugged and resumed her hurried walk.

The voice came again—louder, clearer, and more urgent: *"Run, Dolores, Run!"* Just then, she felt a shove in the small of her back, forcing her to either fall or run. She bounded forward, as if propelled by the hand of a giant, just as a lightning bolt struck the elm tree she'd been passing under.

Out of the corner of her eye, Dolores saw the huge tree topple behind her with a deafening crash. Her ears vibrated with the sounds of falling brick, breaking limbs, and smashing glass as the tree slammed into the little one-room schoolhouse and brought it crumbling to the ground. When at last the terrifying sounds subsided, Dolores realized she was lying facedown on the sidewalk, pinned under the outer branches of the fallen tree. She lay there, alone and frightened and unable to move, for several minutes.

Finally, a woman ran toward her, calling, "Are you all right, little girl?" The woman, whom Dolores had never seen before, lifted the branches and helped Dolores to her feet. She explained that she'd been walking down the street when she'd heard a loud crack and saw the tree smash into the schoolhouse.

"Are you sure you're all right?" she asked again.

Aside from a few scratches on her arms and legs, Dolores was unharmed.

"Do you live far from here?" the woman asked. "Would you like me to walk you home?"

"No, thank you," Dolores answered. All she wanted was to be inside her own house again.

Still dazed, Dolores hurried home. She told her mother what had happened—about the voice calling her name and telling her to run, about the powerful hand that had pushed her out of harm's way. But her mom was the only one she was able to tell her story to. In the weeks that followed, as her classmates chattered about the fallen schoolhouse, she maintained a strange silence about her experience. It even curbed her daring adventures for a while.

Dolores thought and thought about the voice in the storm. She wondered about the invisible hand that had nudged her away from the elm's crushing trunk. Then one day, as she lay on her back in the grass gazing up at the billowy clouds in the blue-blue sky, she figured it out: God had cared so much about her that he'd sent an angel to save her life.

She has never doubted her miracle or been afraid of life's storms since.

~Dolores Martin

Grandpa's Suitcase

The forecast reads: "Fair weather; breeze from the west; rolling sea."

Captain Juham guides his ship, now almost five days out of Le Havre, France, through the midsection of its Atlantic crossing to New York, reported by the ship's owners to be a voyage of 3,255 nautical miles.

Dr. DeCombes and Dr. Meret, the ship's medical officers, tend to the queasy. Chief Mechanic Lannes checks the ship's gauges. In the dining salon, maitre d'hôtel Pringault prepares to serve dinner to the nearly 2,000 travelers aboard.

The date: June 3, 1920, a Thursday. This is the French Line's *Rochambeau*, a packet boat of 17,417-ton displacement with engines of 13,000 "hevaux" turning her four propellers.

Among the 441 first-class passengers on this voyage is Reuben Prady, a forty-six-year-old resident of Detroit, Michigan, originally from Riga, Latvia, by way of New York City and Boston. Grandpa. Father of my mother Mildred, and her younger brother Harry, and her older brother Ben, a lifelong bachelor who lived with his parents.

That evening aboard the *Rochambeau,* Grandpa dines on consommé, roast pullet with cress salad, and asparagus with mousseline sauce. He has strawberry ice cream for dessert. Two days later, on Saturday, June 5, he has an omelet for lunch. On Sunday, the sixth, it is back to roast pullet for dinner, but the sauce on the asparagus this night is a classic French Argenteuil; the ice cream is chocolate.

What is Grandpa doing on this ship? Where is he going? Where has he been? And how do I know what he had for dinner?

I know all these things because I have Grandpa's suitcase.

It seems small for so large a man; as I remember him he stood about six feet two inches and weighed about 225 pounds. But at two feet by one foot by one-half foot, the dark brown leather suitcase likely was a handy and tractable accomplice whenever Grandpa decided to take a break from Grandma. More than once I had heard my mother talk about the times he had "run away from home."

On the adventure archived in the old suitcase, Grandpa had spent two months in Europe, North Africa, Egypt, and old Palestine. I found the suitcase in Uncle Ben's storage room sixty-six years later, as we cleaned it out following Ben's death in 1986.

Though I had never before seen the suitcase, I somehow knew what it was. Yet I never could have predicted what I discovered inside. I could not have guessed at the joy awaiting me within its casings. Grandpa, bless him, was a collector.

A metallic "yes!" seemed to spring from the lock as I pulled down on the release button and lifted the lid for the first time. I sat down on the floor and reached in, not knowing which of these souvenirs of a life of someone I'd loved to look at first.

Inside I found postcards bearing magical and ancient place names: Marseilles, Bône, Cairo, Port Said, Alexandria, Constantine, Morocco, Jaffa, and Rechoboth.

Grandpa had also brought home pictures of Druse women and of Bedouin riflemen, of the Sphinx, the Pyramids, the streets of Paris, and of ships—likely those that had taken him on leg after leg of his journey.

Excavating Grandpa's travel treasures brought back to me the memory of how he'd taught me to write with a burnt wooden match on the porch ledge while cuddling me in his big arms. I also remembered how I had touched his hand that Thanksgiving night in 1951 as he had sat in a kitchen chair and taken his last breaths. I felt certain that he had purposely left all these things for me to find. I felt certain that he had wanted to share this adventure with me.

The suitcase contained twenty-seven black-and-white postcards, some having faded to an ivory or a buff color, others almost sepia. It also held forty-three color postcards—captivating examples of early 1900s photography and hand-coloring. There, too, were the menus and passenger lists from the *Rochambeau*, along with the passenger list from the Cunard Line's R.M.S. *Mauretania*, bound for Cherbourg and Southampton, on which Grandpa had begun his trip.

Grandpa had also stowed away picture books he'd collected during his travels: from Port Said, from Heliopolis, from Paris, from Jerusalem. One of them even announced with seeming boastfulness: "Souvenir of the Occupation of Jerusalem by the British Troops, Dec. 9, 1917."

I unearthed *Messageries Maritimes*, a fifty-six-page book dating from 1919 offering travelers a map of the Marseilles waterfront, steamship information, and sailing schedules. I believe Grandpa acquired it on his return trip, judging by the use he put it to.

My grandfather had been a sweet man, and as I looked through the book, I found something that seemed to capture the essence of his sweetness. There, between pages 18 and 19 and between pages 30 and 31, lay clusters of tiny flowers he had picked somewhere on the coast of France.

"Milwort," pronounced Dr. Thaddeus Grudzien, a biologist at Michigan's Oakland University, as he looked up at me from his magnifying glass. This group of wildflower, he explained, is found around the world on the edges of forests and on coastal plains. Pink pencil-point petals surround dark red tubular blossoms about a quarter-inch long, and ever so slightly flared, like the tiniest of herald trumpets. I was moved to think of my grandfather picking the flowers right before embarking on his journey home.

Sifting through Grandpa's suitcase, I also found remnants of a personal journey in the form of letters. Included were letters my two sisters, Audrey and Barbara, had written to Grandma, Grandpa, and Uncle Ben in the 1930s from the Lake Michigan resort community where we had spent many summers.

I gave my sisters their letters. Audrey, magnificently retentive and admirably compulsive, tucked hers into one of her mysteriously organized kitchen-desk files. Barbara, born without the collector gene, threw hers away.

Among the letters I also found a small envelope with a purple three-cent Thomas Jefferson stamp. The spasmodic twists of the blue-ink handwriting looked strangely familiar. The return address read: "2750 Tuxedo Detroit 6, Mich."—my childhood home.

I lifted the pointed flap and pulled out a folded card with a panel on the front, in which my name appeared in raised letters. There among Grandpa's mementos, I found a piece of myself: my thank-you note for my grandparents' bar mitzvah present.

"Dear Grandma, Grandpa & Ben," it read, "Your very generous gift is greatly appreciated by me. I shall make very good use of the money in the future. Love, Norman."

Although I suspect that the travel collection I found in Grandpa's suitcase might have some monetary value, the true treasures, to me, are the two bunches of pressed French wildflowers. I can close my eyes and visualize my grandfather putting them into the book to enhance his own memories—and one day, mine. The vision seems to represent to me the depth of our connection.

~Norman Prady

The Colors of Prejudice

Carol glanced at her watch as she pulled into the school parking lot and sighed with relief. It was 2:25 P.M.; Thomas got out of school at 2:30. She'd be waiting at the curbside pick-up spot when the dismissal bell rang. If Carol wasn't there when her son walked out of school, he would panic. Once when she'd been ten minutes late, she'd found him waiting for her in tears.

Carol credited Thomas's insecurity to his having been abandoned by his birth mother in his native Mexico. Carol and her husband George had adopted Thomas when he was three.

Carol sat in the car at the curb, listening to an oldies station and smiling, knowing Thomas would change the radio to a jamming station as soon as he hopped into the car. She spotted him leaving the building, and from the troubled look on his face she could tell that something was wrong. Trailing behind Thomas was a group of boys. One of them shouted something at her son, but Carol couldn't hear what he said. As soon as Thomas spotted his mom, he bolted from the group and jumped in the car.

Locking the door, Thomas shouted, "Get going, Mom. Now!"

As Carol pulled away from the curb, he rolled down the car window and yelled, "Go to hell, nigger!"

"No! Thomas! Stop it! Don't ever say that! I can't believe you said that!" Carol shouted.

Too angry to speak calmly, she drove the rest of the way home in silence. She wondered where he'd heard such a vile word. She wondered what she could say or do to make him understand how wrong it was to say such ugly words.

When Carol parked the car, Thomas reached for the door handle.

"Wait a minute, Thomas. When we go in, I want you to go to your room and think about what just happened."

They got out of the car and walked to the house.

As Carol turned the key in the front door, Thomas blurted out, "You don't know what it's like going to school with them. I don't want to go to that school anymore!"

"You are not changing schools. Dad and I picked that school because we want you to go to a school with children of different racial and ethnic backgrounds," she said, opening the door. "Now go to your room."

Carol walked into the kitchen, and a flood of childhood memories engulfed her. She remembered the countless times her father and uncles had sat around the dining room table, drinking beer, cursing, and slinging racial slurs. Her stomach churned and she trembled, remembering the hate that had filled her childhood home.

Carol knew that ignorance, fear, racism, hate, and violence all went hand-in-hand, and that racism is often passed along from one generation to another. She'd vowed as a girl that it would stop with her. She couldn't let it infect her son. Carol also believed that anger begat anger, and violence begat violence. She was determined to teach her son another way of coping with differences and conflicts. Though she was still upset about his behavior and the horrid memories it had conjured up inside her, Carol forced herself to calm down. She needed to think clearly and find a rational way to deal with this.

Carol poured a glass of milk and placed a few cookies on a paper plate. She picked up a notepad and some markers from the desk and brought them to the kitchen table.

"Thomas, please come into the kitchen," she called.

When Thomas walked into the room, he saw his mom sketching something on the notepad. "Sit down, Thomas, we need to talk," she said. "Please tell me what happened today."

"Those black kids at school are always pushing everybody around. One kid said he was going to 'kick my ass' after school today—for no reason. If you weren't there, he would have done it, too."

"That's no reason for you to use racial slurs."

"But Mom—"

"No buts, young man. You cannot—will not— say those kinds of words to anyone, ever. I mean it," Carol said. She paused, using silence to reinforce the gravity of her words. "Calling people names doesn't solve anything. Being hateful to someone who's been hateful to you just builds more hate. Remember the golden rule?"

"Yeah, I guess."

"Hate leads to violence, and then people can get hurt or even killed."

Placing the picture she'd drawn in front of her son, Carol asked, "What is this?"

Thomas looked at the rectangular box with three colored circles. "A traffic light."

"Yes, but they're also the colors of prejudice."

"Shouldn't they be black and white?"

"Thomas, as you get older you'll learn that nothing is black and white. Also, there are many more colors of people than black and white," she said.

"But how come they're the colors of prejudice?"

"Well, red is the color of hate and anger. Amber is the color of caution and fear. Green is the color of envy and jealousy."

"I don't understand, Mom."

Carol searched for a way to put it into perspective.

"I was about your age during the Civil Rights movement in the mid-1960s. There were marches, fights between blacks and whites, and riots. Some of my relatives hated blacks and Jews, and their anger and hate scared me. But I also remember being afraid of blacks for no reason.

"When I was little," she went on, "my dad and uncles were good people in my eyes. They never hurt anyone or broke any laws. At family gatherings they would talk about why they hated blacks and Jews and say nasty things about them. I didn't understand and it made me feel scared and bad inside, but I didn't question it, because they were the grownups."

"Why did they hate black people?"

"I think because they thought black people were very different from them. They looked and talked differently; they had different customs and manner-isms. And that made my dad and uncles afraid."

She gave Thomas a moment to absorb what she'd said.

"I think my family was also envious of Jews, because some of the Jewish people in our town, through hard work and ambition, had become well educated and wealthy. My family's jealousy made them feel inferior, and that made them feel threatened."

Thomas looked at his mother intensely, trying to decode all she was saying.

"Are you saying Grandpa was a racist?"

"I'm saying that Grandpa and many other people were confused and scared and jealous, and they let those feelings turn into anger and hate. I believe prejudice is fear and envy camouflaged as anger. And I believe fear and envy come from ignorance, from not really knowing or understanding the other person."

"How come you didn't turn out like Grandpa?"

"When I was about thirteen something happened that made me think about all these things. You know my family is Catholic and I went to a Catholic grade school, right?"

"Uh-huh."

"Well, when I was in seventh grade I transferred

to public school, where I met my best friend, Gail. Gail's family was Protestant. One day I went with Gail to her aunt's house. Everyone was sitting around the kitchen table, drinking beer and saying bad things about Catholics. One of the things I remember them saying was a pregnant woman would be crazy to have a baby in a Catholic hospital."

"Why would they say that?"

"Years ago if there was trouble when a baby was born, doctors in Catholic hospitals would make sure the baby was taken care of first, and sometimes the mother died because of it. Gail's relatives were angry about that; they had lots of other mean things to say about Catholics, too. It really upset me."

"Did you tell them to shut up?"

"No, I just listened. When I got home, I told Grandpa what had happened. He told me Gail's relatives were just ignorant and that I shouldn't pay any attention to what they said. I looked at him and said, 'But Dad, they talk about Catholics like you talk about niggers.' Until then, I had never said that word. Grandpa was silent and a sad look came over his face. He hugged me and said I should remember that there are many blacks who are good people and never to judge someone by the color of his skin."

"Did Grandpa stop saying that word?"

"No, but I stopped judging people by the color

of their skin," she said. "But sometimes I still have trouble not being afraid of people who are different from me."

Carol took her son's hand in hers. He studied the contrast between her creamy white hand and his light brown one.

"Mom, are you afraid of me?"

Carol hugged her son tightly. "No, I love you very, very much. But I'm afraid of what might happen to you and the world if people don't stop hating each other for being different."

Reaching over, Thomas grabbed the markers and pad. He carefully removed the page with her drawing from the pad and began making a series of arches, each a different color, on a fresh page. When he was finished, he pushed his picture across the table to Carol.

"What's this, Mom?"

"A rainbow," she said.

"No, those are the colors of hope and love."

Carol looked into her son's big brown eyes. "Why is that?"

"Well, when people see a rainbow it gives them hope that the rain is going to stop and the sun is going to shine again. And that makes people happy."

"Oh, I see," she nodded. But her young son had more to teach her.

"It takes the six other colors to get the violet arc in the center of the rainbow. All the different colors are beautiful, but they all have to come together in the middle to make a rainbow. And that takes love."

Smiling, Carol picked up Thomas's rainbow and laid it on top of her drawing. "You're right, Thomas. And rainbows always come after a storm."

~M. A. Kosak

The White Dress

Kitty gave her hips a little twist and smoothed out her white dress before plopping down on the back porch. She was supposed to keep her new dress clean, but she didn't care—she hated the white dress with its puffed sleeves and scratchy lace around the neck. She hunched forward and, propping her chin in her hand, chewed on her last good fingernail. She didn't think anyone inside would notice her absence; in fact, she believed that as far as the grownups were concerned, she might as well have been invisible.

When Kitty had first seen the dress, she had been standing in the doorway of the bedroom watching Aunt Mildred shake it loose from the tissue paper.

"Anna, the child is too young to wear black. She's only eight years old; she doesn't need to be dragged into this tragedy. Children aren't supposed to mourn;

they forget. This will do nicely for the funeral as well as for the piano recital, and it'll give her something to wear this summer."

"They're talking about me," Kitty thought. "Hey! I'm right here. Why do grownups talk like kids can't hear?"

Each day of the wake, Kitty had stood with her mother and fourteen-year-old brother next to the bronze casket placed before the front windows in the parlor. Her legs had ached from the pins and needles shooting up from her toes curled up in her white shoes. She had stood motionless, her eyes hot and dry, unable to understand why she shouldn't "mourn the dead." The white dress had made her different, as if she were sealed in a bright bubble that floated in the middle of a forest of black dresses and suits. As she watched the dark procession file past her father's casket, it had reminded her of blackbirds sitting in a row on the back fence, bobbing and cackling. Each person would lean over the casket; some would shake their heads while others would dab at their eyes. Then they would turn toward her mother and brother. Kitty would hold her breath, knowing that next they would swoop down to pat the top of her head or to press their wet cheeks against her own. She would become invisible again as they talked over her head.

"Poor thing—no insurance, you know," whispered a short woman in black wearing a straw hat with a crooked veil. "It's awful—particularly the way he went."

"How terrible for Anna—first her brother six months ago and now her husband," answered a stout woman with thick arms and damp, red cheeks.

"What a terrible way to go. This could scar a child for life."

"*Shhh*. The child is listening."

Kitty had shivered and tried to understand the voices. What were they talking about? She had felt a hand on her shoulder and looked up to see her grandfather staring at the two women with a deep frown on his face. He had smoothed Kitty's hair and said softly, "Why don't you go out to the kitchen and get a little something to eat?"

She had walked into the kitchen and found it empty, the table piled high with plates and bowls of food that would later be taken to the dining room for the family and guests. The sight of the food had made Kitty's stomach churn, and she had darted out the door to the back porch.

She sat alone on the top step. The cement backyard was empty except for two long boxes standing next to the woodshed. Kitty and her grandfather had planted tomatoes and other vegetables in the boxes last year. Now everything was dried up and dead. A lone bird circled the boxes, hesitated, and then flew off.

"I wish I could go, too," Kitty whispered.

The sound of the screen door slamming behind her made Kitty turn to look. Her grandfather was standing on the porch. He carried a chicken leg wrapped in a white paper napkin and grunted as he sat down next to her.

"Too many people in there. I see you need a little quiet, too." He pointed the chicken leg towards her. "Want a bite?"

"No thanks, Boompop."

Kitty liked her grandfather. He didn't talk much. When he came home from work, he would just sigh a lot while he took off his shoes, then would often fall asleep on the couch after dinner. Once in a while he would frown and twist his mustache when everyone got too noisy at the dinner table, but most of the time he was very nice. When her father had been away, Kitty and Boompop would do things together, like making root beer and riding the trolley to get Sunday night's bread from the bakery across town. She glanced toward the flower boxes and remembered how her grandfather hadn't even gotten angry when she'd mixed up the vegetable seeds last spring.

"We're gonna eat 'em together," he'd said. "Guess they all can grow together."

His heavy dark suit brushed against her bare arm. It looked tired, she thought—not like her dad's suit. Daddy had always looked like he was going to a party, with his striped necktie and a clean white handkerchief in his breast pocket that was "only for show and not for blow."

When Dad would come home on weekends from his job in New York City, Kitty would run down the street to meet him. He would lift her up on his shoulders and rock from side to side like a horse, while Kitty tightened her arms around his neck. At night, he would sit on her bed. His stories of magic and fairies and faraway places had opened the door to a secret world where everything was pretty and people were always happy. Kitty suddenly shivered as a terrible thought crept into her mind: Dad's gone and he took his stories with him.

Her grandfather coughed, interrupting her thoughts.

"About time we start looking for new seeds for the garden. I have to get some topsoil first, so we can give the little seeds a chance to take hold and grow. Little seeds need lots of tending."

He pulled a rumpled handkerchief from his back pocket. "Lord, Kitty, the way you're squirming around, that dress won't be fit to wear." He spread his handkerchief next to her on the porch. "Here. Sit on this. It will keep you clean so your Aunt Mildred won't fuss about your dress gettin' dirty."

Kitty looked at the handkerchief, which was almost as dirty as the porch. That must be his blow one, she thought.

"I don't want to wear this dress after tomorrow, after we come back from the cemetery. I don't want to wear it ever again." She glanced sideways and saw Boompop raise his white bushy eyebrows and pull his lips together the way he did when he was thinking about something.

"It's a nice dress, very pretty. Your Aunt Mildred looked a long time to find it." He patted her knee with a heavy lined hand that looked like a washboard. "Why don't you like it?"

Kitty stared straight ahead, afraid to look at him. Her insides were starting to squirm again, and she felt her heart beating faster. She knew her face was getting red and tried to bite her lips, but the words she'd pushed deep down inside her were rising in her throat.

"Why couldn't I have a black dress like everyone else? I can't mourn in a white dress. I heard Aunt Mildred say so." Kitty's words were getting all mixed up with hiccups. "Why do I have to forget my dad? Why can't I feel bad, too?"

Kitty felt her grandfather lift her up and wrap his arms tightly around her. The painful bubble inside her began to melt like ice cream on a summer day. She pressed her forehead against his chest, gradually feeling safe in this comfortable familiar place. Her father had always smelled like his shaving lotion, and sometimes whiskey, but Boompop's suit reminded her of the furnace when he started the fire on cold mornings and the open pack of Life Savers he always carried in his pocket. There were other smells: of his pipe and the cleaning fluid her grandmother used on his jacket. She clung tightly to him. All the tears she had tried to blink away began to spill over and roll down her face.

"Ah dear. My poor dear," her grandfather murmured. "Poor little thing. We don't know your hurt. Ah, Kitty, just because grownups are bigger and older doesn't make us any smarter. Your Aunt Mildred was trying to protect you, to keep you from being so hurt, but we can't protect you all the time."

Kitty looked up into his gentle, sad eyes and saw that they were wet and red-rimmed.

"All living beings with a soul and feelings mourn when they suffer a loss; it makes no difference what color they wear," he said.

"Mourning is like having a sore that takes time to heal. You cry all you want, kitten. Tears are nature's way of helping heal that sore. Sometimes the sad and happy things get mixed up together, and it takes time to sort 'em out so that the hurt will go away. Then we put the sadness of missing someone in a secret place inside, like hiding a special present under the bed at Christmas. We wrap it up in a special magic called love.

"It's love that makes the hurt fade, and it's love that keeps that person with us. Your dad loved you more than anything. I figure your aunt thought that because your dad liked to see you dressed bright and pretty, seeing you in that nice dress would make him happy. He's lookin' down on you, Kitty. We gotta believe they're always looking down on us. Don't you ever forget him."

He looked up at the sky, and Kitty saw his mustache quiver. *He's got a hurt, too,* she thought.

"Are you still mourning Uncle Bob?" Kitty asked hesitantly.

"Sometimes, Kitty. He was my only boy, and I try to remember how he looked when he laughed and the nice things he did. Remembering helps keep him close."

He gave a deep sigh that seemed to come up from his shoes, and Kitty watched two tears roll down his lined face. She reached up and gently brushed the tears away, patting and stroking his face the way she stroked her doll when she played mother. She felt older somehow. Her grandfather was the oldest person she knew, but he was sitting here next to her with tears on his face and talking to her like she was a grownup. She was not invisible to Boompop.

"Wanna blow, child?" he asked, picking up the handkerchief from the porch and holding it out to her.

She stared at the wrinkled, soiled cloth. Her grandfather nodded and grinned. He reached up, pulled the clean handkerchief from his breast pocket, and handed it to her.

"Isn't this your show one, Boompop?"

She watched his eyes crinkle and a little smile spread over his face as he chuckled. "Depends on how bad a person needs it."

Kitty took the handkerchief and dabbed at her eyes. Leaning closer, she smoothed it across his cheeks. She dusted pieces of lint from his suit with her fingertips, straightened his necktie, and then fitted the damp handkerchief back in his breast pocket.

"Don't feel bad, Boompop. I'll take care of you."

"Kitty," he said softly, "we'll take care of each other."

~Helene LeBlanc

An Angel's Voice

I was tired. Bone tired. Tired of working all day and then watching my four-year-old granddaughter every night while my daughter, Kealy, worked.

They lived in a ground-floor apartment next to the house where I lived in a small upstairs apartment, made smaller by the array of toys and toddler clutter constantly underfoot. I got off work at 5:00 P.M., and my daughter had to be at work by 6:00, so we usually ended up with less than an hour to make quick work of supper, catch up on conversation, and hand over Phoenix, my granddaughter. Because Kealy's shift ended too late to wake Phoenix and take her home, my granddaughter usually spent the night with me. We slept together in the same small bed, and each night I lost a little bit more sleep as she kicked and squirmed out of the covers or cuddled so close to me

I couldn't move. In the mornings, my daughter and I made another quick, sleepy exchange of Phoenix before I went to work.

On that particular bone-tired night, my daughter wasn't scheduled to work. So earlier in the day, I had begged for a night of solitude to catch up on housework and rest.

I cleaned house, took a long bath, lit candles, turned on music, and stretched out on my bed to read. Fatigue, however, soon overtook me, and I fell asleep, book in hand. Not long after, I heard pounding at the door.

"Bamma! Bamma!" called Phoenix from outside.

"Damn it," I said to myself, waking up from what had been a nice dream, annoyed that my daughter had ignored my request for an evening alone. I considered not responding to the knocking and calls, but the knocking got louder and the calls more persistent.

"Bamma, Bamma, Bamma!"

"Okay, hold on," I called, moving from the bedroom into the hallway and toward the front door.

That's when I saw the flames. The candles I'd lit earlier had ignited the lampshade on a table in the hall between the door and me. The flames licked the wall, which was scorched and would soon ignite.

"Wait a minute," I screamed at the door. "I've got a problem!"

I grabbed the flaming lampshade, hurried to the kitchen, and doused it with water in the sink.

Then, I rushed to open the door to let in Kealy and Phoenix, but no one was there. Assuming they had given up on me, I went back inside and dialed my daughter's number.

"I couldn't answer your knock," I told her. "I had a fire in the hallway."

"What are you talking about?" Kealy asked.

"Well, I heard you knocking on my door and Phoenix calling for me, but I'd fallen asleep, and candles had caught a lamp on fire, and I had to put it out."

"Mom," Kealy said, "you told us to leave you alone tonight. We weren't at your door. We've been here all night."

The next day I told my friend Sue about the fire and how positive I'd been that I'd heard Phoenix calling.

"It wasn't like I *thought* I heard her, I *did* hear her just as if she was standing in front of me," I insisted. "I was sure of what I'd heard and sure I'd find them standing outside my door when I opened it."

"Maybe you did. Maybe you have an angel watching over you. Maybe the angel knew the only voice you would listen to was your granddaughter's," Sue said.

"I don't know," I said.

"Think about it: Would you have answered the door if it had been anyone else?"

Think about it I did. And the answer was, no. I would not have responded to any other voice that night. Had I not heard my granddaughter's urgent call at that moment, I would have soon been trapped in a room with no exit and might have perished in a fire.

I thought about other things as well, like how what had once seemed like the worst event of my life, the unexpected pregnancy of my then sixteen-year-old daughter, had turned into the surest blessing of my life. Although it had taken some doing to make it all work, it was working.

I also thought about what a wonderful mother Kealy had become and what a special little soul Phoenix is. She came, I believe, to show my daughter and me how strong we, and love, are.

Perhaps I do have an angel looking out for me, a guardian who speaks to me silently or in the only voice I'm able to hear when I'm too tired or too frightened to listen to my own soul.

It's been two years since the fire in the hallway. Kealy changed jobs and only works days now.

Phoenix attends a great school; she no longer calls me "Bamma" and she doesn't stay with me as often. I have plenty of time to paint, read, sleep, and enjoy my daughter and my granddaughter.

Now, whenever life threatens to overwhelm me, I listen for my angel, whispering from somewhere within my soul, waking me up to what is really important.

~Stephanie Barrow

The Greatest
Christmas Gift

One of my most cherished Christmas memories involves a Christmas when the only gifts I received came without gift-wrap.

My mother gave birth to my new brother, Richard, on November 22, 1948. When she brought him home from the hospital, she put him in my lap, saying, "I promised you a baby, and here he is." What an honor! I had turned four just one month earlier, and none of my friends had a baby of their own. Maybe Mother didn't intend to mean the baby belonged to me, but I interpreted her words as such, and love filled my heart for the little red creature squirming in my arms.

From that day forward, I spent hours by Richie's crib, studying his wrinkled little face or playing with his tiny fingers. I marveled at my living baby doll and even dreamed of him at night. I sang to him.

I entertained him with stories and told him over and over how much I loved him. He gurgled to me, and I delighted in his every move and expression. I could hardly get to sleep at night, because I was so eager for morning, when I could sit near my very own baby again. I could barely lift him, but I learned to change his diapers with a great deal of guidance and assistance from Mother.

Richard had been home but a few weeks when he developed a cough. I dreaded the sound of his shallow breaths and the sight of his runny nose. He slept more than he had before, and I would anxiously sit nearby, waiting for him to wake up.

One morning I found his crib cold and empty. I ran back to the room I shared with my six-year-old sister, screaming that someone had stolen my baby. My sister rocked me in her arms as she explained that Richie had gone to the hospital to get well, but would be home again soon. From then on, my twelve-year-old sister prepared our meals while Mother and Dad spent endless hours at the hospital, keeping vigil over the infant with pneumonia. I overheard whispered conversations with ominous words and phrases, such as "hopeless," "pitiful," "dying," and "so young."

One December evening, my father gathered my two older sisters, my older brother, and me in the living room. We sat around in a semicircle, the way we often sat when the family played "musical instruments." Dad sat on the piano bench, as usual, but facing us rather than the keyboard. We kids sat empty-handed, instead of holding our usual "instruments" of wooden spoons and kitchen pots.

"We've got to tighten our belts," Dad told us.

I thought of the sashes on the dresses Mother sewed for me and wondered why I had to tie them tighter. I kept listening, trying to understand. As my father spoke, his eyes filled with tears. I'd never seen him cry before, and I felt bewildered by the sight.

"Don't expect any presents this year. If your baby brother lives, that'll be Christmas enough," Daddy said. "We should all be happy for what we have and hope that Richard comes home soon, strong and healthy."

I could not comprehend what my father had tried to tell us. I missed my baby terribly, but the thought of the upcoming holidays cheered me a little. How could my brother's illness affect Christmas? Santa Claus had always filled our stockings with apples, oranges, and walnuts. Nothing could change that.

Richard's hospitalization changed many things. Dad did not bring home a Christmas tree. Mother did not sew or crochet gifts. Every night we kids ate simple meals unlike the ones Mother usually cooked.

Dinner conversation contained a few chuckles, but nothing like the raucous laughter we used to enjoy when the whole family gathered together. With Richard in the hospital, we youngsters would usually sit around the kitchen table looking quietly and helplessly at each other as we ate our dinner, which often consisted of just cold cereal and milk.

As the days dragged on, I grew fearful of asking about my baby. Nobody mentioned his name anymore. Silence had replaced the laughter that used to float through the house. With Mother and Dad still at the hospital on Christmas Eve, my ten-year-old brother Barry supervised while we kids hung our stockings—including a small one for Richard—placing a name at the top of each. Though we had no tree and no presents, I knew Santa would take care of filling our socks.

The phone rang early on Christmas morning. Dad jumped out of bed to answer it. My father always bellowed into the telephone, as if to ensure that his voice would travel the distance to the other end. From my bedroom I heard him say, "What? He's all right?" He hung up and yelled upstairs. "The hospital said we can bring Richard home!"

"Thank God!" I heard Mother cry.

From the upstairs window, I watched my parents rush out to the car; I had never seen them so happy.

I also felt full of joy. What a wonderful day! My baby would soon be back home, and my Christmas goodies waited below.

I skipped downstairs and into the living room. I gasped. The socks hung exactly as we had left them, lifeless and flat. Behind me, I heard footsteps. I turned to find Barry, also still in his pajamas. I grabbed his flannel sleeve. "There's nothing there," I sobbed.

He hugged me and looked over my shoulder at the mantel. "Did you look closely?"

I told him I didn't have to. I could see from where I stood.

"Well, look." He walked to the fireplace and pulled down a note.

I sniffed. "What does it say?"

He read to himself and nodded.

I moved closer, curious. He pointed to lettering that looked suspiciously like his own handwriting. "This explains everything."

"What?" I asked through tears.

Barry cleared his throat. "It says right here: 'These stockings may look empty, but they are filled with love.'"

~Bobbie Christmas

Hidden Treasure

My ten-year-old friends and I followed Fred around all summer. That strange old man dressed in old-fashioned suits smelling of mothballs and with an erratic haircut that exposed the scars where his left ear should have been, seemed to endlessly wander the dusty streets of our small village. We jeered and laughed at him the way callow youths often react to those who are different from themselves, never noticing or understanding the perpetual look of shame and pain on his weathered face. To us, Fred was the village idiot and a scapegoat for all of our feelings of inadequacy.

It came as a shock to me, then, while I sat crying one day in the broad branches of the big oak tree beside Brock's hardware store, to hear Fred's rough voice calling, "Don't cry, child. Life's too short for tears."

My father had just told me we were moving. Dad, a sergeant in the Canadian Armed Forces, was being posted to Ottawa, Canada's capital city. Although he'd broken the awful news to me gently, nothing could have prepared me for the shock of having to leave everything I'll ever know. I was deeply saddened at the thought of leaving my home and my friends.

Fred called me down from the tree, and despite my earlier conviction that he was someone to be feared, I came. His voice, the empathy in it, seemed to pull me out of the branches and to him. Looking back, my response seems strange, given my earlier behavior toward Fred. But some instinct within me sensed the good in him.

He said, "Come, child. I have something to cheer you up: buried treasure."

So I followed.

I followed Fred for the rest of that summer, seeing the village through his aging eyes, hearing the stories of his life, filling in the whys and hows that had been a mystery I'd had no interest in discovering before. Of course, I consequently became a pariah to my friends, but I suppose I was subconsciously trying to pull away from them, to buffer the pain of our eventual separation.

Fred had been in the war—the Great War. That's what he told me.

"My ear—I lost it fighting," he said shyly.

There he stopped, offering no further explanation. But he showed me several medals and ribbons, hidden in his trunk among heavy, scratchy, out-of-date suits polka-dotted with mothballs. Those were his only clothes. They looked 100 years old to me.

What of his chopped hair? Well, he barbered himself, he explained.

"It's my eyes. Can't see too well," he said, then looked away and reddened. "I do my best."

His best was terrible, but I couldn't tell him that.

Then there were the photo albums: with pictures of Fred as a fat baby in a long, lacy dress; as a boy of about my age, in knickers; and as a strapping man in an army uniform, looking very proud and oh so young.

Fred was a very good cook. He had a large garden in his backyard, where he grew tomatoes, turnips, onions, cabbage, green beans, and carrots. I helped him hoe his plot, the two of us wearing men's straw hats—mine too large and falling off whenever I bent over. To this day, his vegetable soup remains the best I've ever tasted.

At that age I understood little of finances. To me, Fred was an eccentric. To the other children, he was just plain weird, a freak. I'd sometimes think: How can he live like this, with so little and everything so old? Are these shabby relics and handful of medals and ribbons the extent of his treasure?

In time, I came to understand that Fred's "buried treasures" consisted of the beauty and wonder he saw in everything around him.

During that first week with Fred, he pointed to an upper window in one of the old white clapboard houses while we wandered around the village and asked, "See the cat, child?"

Mrs. McDermitt's white cat, Pumpkin, sat like a fat ball of cotton in the lace-curtained bedroom window, staring at the big chestnut tree in the front yard.

"Follow her eyes," Fred instructed. "Try to see what she sees."

But I was unaccustomed to seeing deep into things, to delving beyond the brick wall of a house or the skin of another child. Eventually, however, the leaves began to part and my eyes took in a small nest with a tiny bird sitting on it.

"She's a jenny," Fred whispered. "A little jenny wren—very shy. You don't see one often."

Indeed, I had never seen one before that day. Completely unaware of Pumpkin or of us, the small bird alternately preened herself and sang of the joys of motherhood. We must have stood for a quarter of an hour watching her.

I remembered how, in the days before I came to know Fred, I would see him staring at things, standing as still as if playing statues for what seemed like hours. To all of us children, his seemingly vacant state had offered proof of what we thought he was: a fool.

During those next few weeks with Fred, I, too, did a lot of foolish staring. Once, I stood staring at a wall of jewels—garnets encrusted in the granite bank of the Nottawasaga River, a bank that until then I had thought of only as a useful diving-off place. Another time my gaze soaked up a sea of Michaelmas daisies, their green and purple bright in the summer sun, which before had seemed only a field of weeds to me.

That summer of my tenth year, I discovered a new wonder and fresh delight in everything I saw. And I carried that enchantment with me long after I had said goodbye to Fred and to all my other, younger, friends.

Fred is gone now. He passed on five years after I left the village where I grew up and where I learned that child and grownup can be synonymous terms, if only you look at the world in Fred's special way. I hope that I left something with Fred, too, to hold him over those five years, for he had given me so much.

I believe that my relationship with Fred ultimately influenced my choice of a husband: for while the man I married is not the handsomest of men, he is certainly the kindest and most generous. His wisdom sometimes astounds me. And his love—well, let me just say that I consider myself to be one of the luckiest women on God's earth.

We have a dog—an ugly dog. His hair stands up in clumps, and he lost an ear in a fight long before we took him in. Our motley mutt appreciates this world's treasures with every breath of his slightly arthritic body, charging ahead of us to seek them out whenever we walk through the fields and woods behind our home. We call him Fred.

~*Joy Hewitt Mann*

The Sweet Pea

A blanket of depression enveloped me when my lungs failed while I was recovering from heart surgery. Unable to do anything or go anywhere, I felt lost and hopeless, wondering what the point was of continuing in that dreary and lonely existence.

The lung problem developed shortly after my surgery to have a defective heart valve replaced. My lungs had always been my weak spot, and the added strain of the valve replacement had pushed my condition over the edge. I had no idea how serious it had become until I suddenly required supplemental oxygen twenty-four hours a day.

It was bad enough having to walk around my home with a breathing tube connecting me to a machine that converted room air to oxygen; there was no way I was going out in public tethered to a portable oxygen unit—no matter how much the respiratory therapist coaxed me. I felt old, useless, and unattractive. Nothing interested me, none of my usual activities could lift my mood and not being able to return to my job made the situation worse. Soon the thought of leaving home for any reason made me extremely anxious, and I retreated from family and friends. Shopping for groceries became an ordeal, because I was convinced people were staring at me with my portable tank.

When spring arrived, I started my usual preparations for planting a garden, but my heart wasn't in it—I was just going through the motions. Growing and caring for a display of flowers had meant a lot to me ever since I'd been a child working in the yard with my parents. I had always enjoyed feeling the gritty dirt in my hands as I cleaned out the remains of leaves and flowers from the previous year, worked out the lumps in the soil, and turned it over in readiness for the new plants.

The year my life changed so dramatically gave us a spring of crisp weather and bright sunshine almost every day. The feeling of promise in the air might have been contagious, but I didn't find it catching. I shut myself off, stayed indoors as much as possible, and closed my ears to the calling of spring. Old habits die hard, though, and occasionally I went outside to work in the garden. Soft breezes brushed my face as

I carried out the familiar chores, but I barely noticed anything other than the oxygen tank I carted with me.

As always, the perennials sprang miraculously back to life after having looked completely dead the month before. First came the crocuses, and then the tulip and daffodil shoots poked out of the ground. With no effort whatsoever on my part, their cheery blooms soon brightened the garden. I remained depressed, however, doing only the most perfunctory upkeep on the garden.

A few years before, I had planted sweet peas by the garage and had attached a net to the side of the garage as a support for them to grow on. They liked the location and produced copious amounts of flowers, so I continued planting them every year after that. In the year of my discontent, when what little I did was done on automatic pilot, I went ahead with the sweet peas. It involved little work, and enthusiasm wasn't required, so I placed the seeds along the full length of the garage. As the new plants appeared, I tended to them absent-mindedly.

One day as I weeded the garden around the sweet peas and gently guided the newly emerging plants onto the net, I noticed something unusual. Around the corner, in a cracked section of the path, something was growing and it wasn't a weed. Look-

ing closer, I saw that it was a lone sweet pea, probably from a seed I had dropped during planting. Bits
of cracked concrete had sunk below the main path,
and the plant had had to work around them to
find some space to get through, but it had managed
somehow. The seedling's efforts to find its way to
light had markedly deformed the stalk; however, the
plant looked healthy so I decided to leave it alone.
Because there was nowhere for it to climb, I figured
it wouldn't grow much more and might even die.
I didn't have the energy to care much one way or the
other.

It soon became apparent that I had misjudged
the little plant's urge to survive. It kept growing until
it was long enough for one of its tendrils to attach to
a nail jutting out from the garage wall. As the plant
grew, it found other things to grasp onto: a piece
of loosened paint, a section of spider web, a twig
that was stuck in the remnants of a web. It wasn't
receiving the same attention as the other plants, so
it still looked rather spindly, and the lower part of it
remained tortuously twisted, but the plant was alive
and growing.

A piece of the ice encasing my heart chipped
off as I looked at the misfit sweet pea. After I put
a couple of nails and some string on the wall so it
wouldn't have to look so hard for something to grasp

onto, the plant seemed bigger and healthier every time I looked at it.

To my utter amazement, that remarkable little sweet pea eventually sprouted buds—lots of them. Then came the morning when I stepped outside and was greeted by something I barely even recognized: the orphan sweet pea was covered with the best-looking blooms of any plant in my garden. The lavishly large flowers were a rich shade of red. I walked over and noticed how straight and tall the plant had grown after its initial twisted start. I marveled at how proudly it wore its blaze of flowers. Leaning over to smell the blossoms, I murmured to the plant, "Message received. Thank you."

Then I stood up straight and smiled for the first time in months.

~Judi Chapman

Home Place

Aunt Molly's visit with us was drawing to a close and she had shown no sign of wanting to go back to the old family farm, just a few miles from ours, where she and Papa had grown up. Mama and Papa had promised Aunt Molly that they wouldn't broach the subject during her visit, but they were hoping she'd come to her own decision to go see the old place.

When I asked Papa once why he sometimes wanted me to go over there with him, even though nobody lived there anymore, he had said that it was part of our history, who we are. I said that I thought we already knew that. He tried to explain that it made him feel whole, connected, all of a piece—that I'd understand some day when I was older, which is what my parents always said.

Aunt Molly hadn't been back to the farm, or even

these parts, since she'd eloped as a teenager, riding on the horse behind Uncle Cyrus and hanging onto him for dear life, on their way to the preacher. "Like Indians were after them," the townspeople said.

"Little pitchers have big ears," Mama often said, and I knew she meant me. With no brothers or sisters, listening in was how I learned things—interesting stuff, like about Aunt Molly eloping.

My folks had been coaxing her to come for years. They said it would do her good to go on back and make her peace. She had always replied that she had Cyrus and the boys to look after—that she was busy and content with her life on their Kansas wheat ranch.

"Even now she can't let go," Papa said, reading the letter in which she at last agreed to come. "She says that she knows it's not Christian, but she can't forgive."

Mama frowned at Papa and tossed a look in my direction. I turned quickly back to my Elsie Dinsmore book so they'd go on talking.

"She says she's coming to see us," Mama said to Papa, "but that she'll never go back to the old farm. Do you think she means it?"

"Oh, I'm afraid she does," he replied. "That she's coming here at all is a miracle. She used to say that once she shook the Ohio soil off her heels, she'd never be back."

"Your stepmother, Nel, was alive then."

"Yep. I wish Molly would go back and lay the demons to rest." He paused, sighing deeply. "She thought Pa let Nel work herself to death. Thought he didn't love her."

I glanced up from Elsie to see his eyes all watery, like he'd just sneezed. But he hadn't.

It was a happy reunion for Papa and his sister and a good visit. I liked Aunt Molly from the start. A short, plump lady with blue eyes and auburn hair, like Papa, Aunt Molly livened up the kitchen with her bustling ways and cheery manner. She pitched in with the housework. She helped me carry cookies and cold drinks to the men in the field. And she told me stories about Uncle Cyrus, my big boy cousins, and Kansas.

One evening when I was sitting in my ladder-back rocker by the kitchen fireplace she said, "Come here, child." I went and stood beside her chair, and she took me gently by the arms and moved me around so that I stood in front of her. She fingered my braids and smoothed the hair from my forehead. She looked into my eyes, smiled, and, patting my arm, said, "I just wanted to take a good look at you."

She told me that she had been ten years old, my age, when her mother died.

"Then I took care of your Papa, until . . ." She

clamped her lips tight and gave her head a slight shake, as if she'd bit into a lemon.

"Didn't I do a good job?" And she was all smiles again.

That same night they found the chest. I'd already been sent off to bed, where I lay still and tried to listen to their excited voices downstairs, afraid I was missing something, until sleep finally overtook me. When I came down to breakfast the next morning, they were all at the table, still chattering like chipmunks. Bit by bit I learned what had happened.

They'd been rummaging in the past, Mama said, and Papa and Aunt Molly had gotten to arguing about their father: about what year he'd left Germany, when he came to Ohio.

Mama was the one who'd remembered the chest. A ferocious housekeeper, she'd come across it when she'd been turning out the parlor. Papa recollected that his father had given it to him shortly before he died—that and the old Seth Thomas clock on the mantel.

"Open the box after I die," Grandpa had said.

Papa said he'd tried, but it had been locked. He'd figured he'd hunt around for the key, but then he'd forgotten all about it. Last night Aunt Molly had taken a notion that the key was in the clock.

"I don't know why," she said, "the idea just came over me."

Next to the big key for winding the clock they had found two smaller ones.

When they opened the chest they saw that it was filled with papers—accounts mostly; their father had been a stickler for records. There were also wills, receipts, some letters, and the family's original land grant from 1813. Mama, Papa, and Aunt Molly had stayed up reading the papers until they had finally given out and fallen into their beds.

The next morning they had decided to wait for me before going on with it. I forced down a few bites of porridge and was the first one into the parlor, where I waited by the chest.

"Inside the chest is a secret drawer with its own key," Aunt Molly told me. "We waited to open it until you could be present."

We all leaned forward as Papa pulled out the chest, set it on the mantel, unlocked it, and inserted the smaller key into the inner compartment.

The drawer didn't want to open. Papa jiggled it a bit, then very gently slid it open. Inside was a faded black box with unreadable gold printing. Papa carried the box to the round center table and placed it there carefully.

He turned to Aunt Molly. "Here, sister. I think you should open this."

Aunt Molly tugged at her apron. She was so slow

I wanted to push her. I leaned over her shoulder and held my breath as she lifted the lid. Inside was something wrapped in a stained, yellowish cloth. She motioned to Papa.

"Here, Benjy. You do it. I've gone all a'dither."

Papa peeled back the cloth, uncovering a gleaming watch—a big old, gold, pocket watch like Papa's, only prettier, with decorations. You'd have thought it was fairy dust the way he slowly turned it over, revealing a big face with strange black figures.

Papa turned the watch back over, and I could see the lettering: BLB.

"Pa's initials," he said. "Wonder if it'll open."

He slid his fingers around the rim and found the catch. I jumped as the lid sprang open, exposing the wheels Papa had told me made the watch go. But there was something else. Deep inside the lid was a lock of hair. Auburn hair. I heard Aunt Molly gasp. She stood white-faced, staring silently.

"It's your hair, Molly, isn't it?" Papa said.

She nodded. "I cut that piece off just before I left. When I started putting my braids up that end would stick out—so I cut it off." Then she started to cry.

That evening when I spotted Aunt Molly heading for the barn, I decided to tag along behind to see what happened. After all, Papa might need me for something.

Papa stopped milking when he saw Aunt Molly. I was right on her heels, so I heard her say it plain as day.

"I want you to take me over to the old farm tomorrow, Benjy. Back home. I'm ready now."

~Mary Helen Straker

Red Two-Seater

It had finally arrived: the day my parents were taking our kids home with them to Tennessee for ten days of quality grandparent time—and the first time Dave and I would be alone since becoming parents—more than ten years ago.

We stood in our driveway at 6:30 in the morning, watching our van, overflowing with our kids and most of their worldly possessions, lumber down the street until it became a distant dot. It took a while, because we have a pretty large van, roughly the size of a strip mall. "Is it a dot yet?" we'd say every so often.

"No, I'd say it's closer to a beach ball. We'd better stick around for another half hour." We waved, dabbing dramatically at our eyes, until we were sure the kids could no longer see us.

Then, party time! Or so I expected.

I stood in the kitchen, surrounded by gooey pancake plates from the big breakfast I had insisted on making, but which everyone had been too excited to eat much of. I gathered bouquets of forks that seconds ago had been in my children's mouths, the four sticky mouths that had just kissed me for the last time in ten days. Now the real tears came.

"My babies are gone, gone, gone," I bawled. "What am I going to do-hoo-hoo-hoo-hoo?"

"Think. Think. What do people without children do?" I spun around, looking for clues. I sat down to read—the same paragraph, four times. I made beds, pressing the kids' pillows to my nose. "Pull yourself together," I told myself. "You're a disgrace to the God-I'd-Kill-for-Such-a-Break Club!"

Like people who've lost the use of one of their senses and find that their other senses become sharper to compensate, I found that without my Sense of Kids, I became acutely aware of my environment. I took notice of little things I hadn't noticed before. Like Dave. "Have you always had that mustache?"

Stranger Dave was everywhere. He'd try putting the moves on me—suddenly his one earthly mission—and I'd say, "Not on the first date."

"Don't you have something to do?" I'd ask.

He'd say, "Yes, but you keep saying 'no.'"

I didn't know how to switch from Mother Person to Wife Person. Dave reminded me that we'd vowed to do all the things during our child-free reprieve that we never would or could with the kids around, to not waste a minute. I just shrugged.

The kids were in excellent hands, but still I wandered through the day, muscles tensed, waiting for something. Finally, in the early evening, my folks phoned; they were in Tennessee, safe, and hadn't felt compelled to leave any children at rest stops. I took the first breath of the day.

"It's Saturday night," Dave said. "It would be illegal to sit home."

"Oh I don't know . . . " I pictured the kids unpacking, finding their pajamas and the stuffed animals they would sleep with on this first night of many away from me.

"Come on," Dave insisted. "Remember? We've got The Car."

A spark flickered. *The Car!* In exchange for taking our van, my dad had left us his red two-seater T-topper sportstermobile, which we would drive to Tennessee when we reclaimed our kids.

To say this car is my dad's baby is like saying third-stage labor is somewhat uncomfortable. If it had been up to him, my dad would've had me accompany him to the notary public to sign an affidavit stating

I would never exceed 35 miles per hour; a security guard would be present at all times should I, for some unfathomable reason, leave the vehicle; and I would take the car no further than the city limits.

Doing 90 down the highway toward Canada, out-gunning a driver who was ticked just because I'd cut her off, really helped loosen me up.

Dave and I were at the Ambassador Bridge, which crosses to Canada, when we got our first taste of red car discrimination, which my dad had warned us about. The Canadian customs official grilled us with questions like, "What is your citizenship?" "Where are you going?" "Do you intend to commit any serial murders within our borders?"

We dutifully answered with: "American," "To the casino," and "Not today, we forgot our weapons," which Mr. Customs Official said was very humorous. Then he handed us a document instructing us to pull over for a special vehicle inspection, because the computer had "randomly selected" our red vehicle.

Dave and I exited the car at the inspections bay and stood next to the other menaces to society, try-ing to determine which of us had better mohawks and nipple rings. It seemed amusing in a surreal way, until I remembered my dad's new hunting hobby, which caused my antiperspirant to melt into my shoes. I prayed, "Please let no guns, bloody knives, or dead animal parts that could be mistaken for satanic offerings turn up in my daddy's car!"

We were clean—probably because God had arranged it so we wouldn't spend our first night of freedom "downtown" answering questions under hot lights, when instead we could be trying to figure out how to possibly get ourselves arrested for smuggling Cuban cigars across the border.

Dave bought the cigar at the casino on our way out, about an hour after we had arrived. It had taken me ten minutes to win $160 on a slot machine, after which I declared myself "done," refusing to chance of losing back a nickel of it. I spent the rest of the hour watching Dave internally debate whether his blood was rich enough for the $25-a-hand minimum limit at the card tables or if there was some way he could ditch me. It wasn't, and he couldn't. The $12 cigar was his consolation prize.

We were on a street corner, with Dave about to fire up the stogie, when I stopped him, wondering out loud how one might go about smuggling a Cuban cigar over the border—not that one would do such a thing. After all, Cuban cigars are illegal in the United States, and smuggling contraband would be very, very wrong, even if, for example, one had a brother who was soon expecting his first baby and who would love a good cigar to celebrate it.

Dave admonished me for even thinking of such a thing. And he did *not* make suggestions like, "We could mail it," or "No, hide it in your backpack," or "Under the car seat, next to the bloody knife."

That, of course, meant that anyone passing us on the street corner would *not* have heard us laughing to the point of needing medical attention about what, if we actually did attempt a life of cigar crime, would happen when we got to the border: The U.S. customs official would ask what we wanted to declare, and I, fearless risk taker that I am, as demonstrated by how wantonly I had had my way with a slot machine for ten minutes, would shift my eyes away from the official, sweat pouring off the tip of my nose, while Dave, an equally fearless risk taker, as illustrated by his stunning command of the card tables, would lean over me and scream, "We wish to declare nothing about a Cuban cigar!"

Dave lit the cigar, and we smoked it.

"Ready to go home, Bonnie?" Clyde asked.

Nearly back at the Ambassador Bridge, we encountered an unexpected roadblock. The ever-vigilant Canadian authorities waved through all the vehicles, including tanks capable of launching tactical nuclear weapons, but an officer held up his hand in front of our red car. The officer shined a light through my window. "Have you consumed any alcoholic beverages tonight?"

We were on the road leading directly from a help-yourself-to-the-free-vats-of-alcohol casino, and this man was asking trick questions.

"No?" we guessed, hoping we picked right.

He released us, with a stern warning to turn down our radio. And Agent 007 thought he could wiggle out of trouble. *Mon dieu!* This was getting exciting. The danger, the intrigue! Now, if we could just make it across the border.

Like his Canadian counterpart, the U.S. customs official was tough, savagely interrogating us for upwards of ten seconds with questions like, "Did you have a good time?"

We buckled under the pressure, spilling our guts that, yes, we had fun—thanks to that red car. Getting out in it had helped me to realize we were more than just parents: we were a couple. A couple of weenies who thought a little gambling, drinking, cigar smoking, and a few incredibly minor brushes with the law were really high adventure, sure, but we were a couple. The important thing was, I remembered how to fit into a two-seater again. I hoped the next ten days wouldn't go too fast.

~Denise Wahl

Miracle Fish

All my life I had wanted a fish tank. Yet despite all my pleas during my childhood, it somehow never materialized. As an adult raising five children on a limited budget, I could not afford such a luxury. Nevertheless, my dream persisted.

Then one day I found a thirty-gallon aquarium for five dollars at a garage sale. I rejoiced: my unrequited fish romance would soon be requited! I scrubbed down the old tank, buffed out the scratches, caulked the seams to seal any leaks, and then filled it with water to test it out. Voilà! It held the water just fine. I took the kids on a field trip to the pet store, promising they could help choose the colored gravel and my new aquatic companions. Then my balloon popped! The aquarium setup cost much more than I'd expected, and I went home empty-handed and heavy-hearted.

I set the empty fish tank on the coffee table and used it as a piggy bank, slowly saving up for my scaly pals and their expensive breathing apparatus. Whatever was left over from the grocery budget went into the tank. The kids helped out by having garage sales of their own and by peddling cookies.

After a year, enough change and random dollars had accumulated in the savings tank to enable us to buy the rest of the setup and some fish. My children and I spent hours at the pet store, picking out colored rocks, plants, hiding places, and six perfect fish—one for each of us—as well as all the chemicals and supplies needed to get the fish started in their new home. We chose the healthiest, most robust fish and brought them home in three clear plastic bags. Each child got to hold a bag containing a pair of fish, and they all squealed with delight as they named each fish. The two mollies were appropriately named Molly and Polly, the graumies, Grommet and Bushing, and the silver dollars, Penny and Nickel.

I set the fish loose in the newly cleaned and filled tank. We all spent the evening watching in wonder as they explored their new home. Penny nipped at Polly's tail, but they made up. The kids were happy; I was thrilled. Everything was perfect, except the air bubbles. The air lines were set to blow so strongly that the poor fish were being batted around. When my best efforts failed to correct the problem, I decided to disconnect one of the lines before going to bed so the fish could get a peaceful night's sleep. At eleven o'clock, I unhooked one of the lines, turned off the light over the tank, and bid my new friends good night.

The next morning my husband let me sleep in, as he usually did on Sundays. He got up to get the kids their breakfast and to make coffee. He immediately rushed back to the bedroom, sat on the bed, and gently shook me awake.

"Honey, I'm sorry to wake you, but there is a problem with your fish."

Sleepy-eyed, I asked him what the problem was.

"The water is all gone out of the tank."

Very funny. I had tested the tank for leaks 100 times; that tank was watertight. I flopped over, put my head under the pillow, and said, "Stop teasing me about my fish."

"I'm not joking," he said. "Come look." I peeked up at him and saw he was dead serious. "The weird thing is, the carpet all around the tank is dry."

I sprang out of bed and ran down the hall to the living room. I gasped when I saw my beautiful waterless tank and the lifeless bodies of my fish lying on the rocks. The kids were gathered around the tank, crying and pointing fingers at each other.

I felt the carpet and discovered it was, indeed, dry. How could thirty gallons of water disappear and leave the carpet bone dry? I frantically searched for the reason the water had escaped and where it had escaped to, but came up with nothing. Plagued with guilt at having unknowingly killed my new friends, I called all the pet stores in the Yellow Pages, searching for an answer to the puzzle. Everyone had a different idea of what might have happened. Maybe the tank had overheated and the water had evaporated. Maybe the cats had drunk all the water. My son was convinced aliens had come down from the cosmos and sucked the water from the tank. But none of the explanations panned out, and we were all heartbroken.

After three hours of investigating every possible scenario, I gave up and went out to the backyard to have a private pity party and stepped right into a pool of water next to the sliding-glass door. It didn't take long to discover the source. When I'd unhooked the air line the night before, I'd thrown one end of the tube over the back of the tank. It had evidently landed in the bottom track of the sliding-glass door and had acted as a siphon, emptying the water from the other end of the tube lodged at the bottom of the tank.

With the mystery solved, we began to plan an

elaborate funeral for our new, and newly departed, friends. I fretted over what I could possibly do with the tank and all the accessories now that we had no need for them. My husband, empathizing with our collective pain, offered to buy new fish from our savings. Overjoyed, I threw my arms around his neck and promised to take better care of the next group. We planned to return to the fish store later that day, right after we conducted our six flushable funerals.

We decided that the best way to retrieve the dead bodies for the swift trip down the sewer was to fill the tank with water, let them float to the surface, and scoop them out with a net. I manned the faucet in the kitchen while my daughter directed the hose into the tank.

Suddenly she started screaming, "Mommy, Mommy! They're alive! The fish are alive! It's a miracle!"

I ran back into the room and, as the water continued to stream into the tank, watched in amazement as each fish began to wriggle and shake and spring back to life. By the time the tank was half full, all six of the fish had been resurrected and were swimming happily around the tank. (Molly swam sideways at first, but that soon passed.) They had somehow survived being out of water for more than eight hours! They were indeed miracle fish.

For weeks afterward, the kids made money for new fish by turning my living room into a carnival. They charged the neighborhood kids twenty-five cents apiece to come look at the miracle fish. For fifty cents, they would get to lay their hands on the tank!

I still have most of those original miracle fish. They are my daily reminder that miracles do happen—that even in the worst of circumstances, if you hold your breath long enough, someone will eventually add water.

~Teri Bayus

The Light of Innocence

My daddy worked hard to support our growing family, and we were accustomed to being thrifty. I was the oldest of a brood that would eventually swell to five children. The year I was eight, in the 1940s, we barely had two thin dimes to rub together—a fact that I became painfully aware of as Christmas approached.

Next door to us lived an elderly lady who had a well-shaped cedar tree in her front yard. Every December she would decorate the tree with electric lights that twinkled brightly throughout the crisp winter nights. One day she suggested to me that we decorate our yard, too, so as to help lift the Christmas spirit along our street.

When I told my mom about our neighbor's suggestion, she reminded me that we had only just enough money to buy new decorations for the Christmas tree that would grace our living room. The previous year my brother had accidentally set fire to the Christmas tree with a candle while he was pretending that the tree had blinking lights. Our dad had grabbed a baby blanket from the crib, wrapped it around the burning tree, run to the front door, and thrown the tree into the snow. The decorations had become blackened with soot, so we had had to replace them all with new ornaments.

That year, I was finally old enough to walk alone to the hardware store down the street. I knew the hardware store had Christmas lights, and even though I had no money, I decided to take a walk to the store to look at the lights and see how much they cost. On the way I spotted a dime on the sidewalk. Joy! I picked it up and tucked it into my coat pocket, thinking how lucky I was to have found ten cents. When I reached the store I became temporarily derailed from my mission—first by the exuberant holiday decorations adorning the store and then by the toy section, with its bikes and skates. The salesclerk didn't ask me if I needed any help, understanding that I was just there to look and wish.

The tree lights were kept in the back of the store, away from the potbelly stove that kept the front of the store comfortably warm. I gazed longingly at the strings of outdoor lights that had twelve or fifteen bulbs of varying colors and then looked at their prices. I realized that it didn't matter how many lights were on a string, because I'd never be able to scrape together enough money to buy even the smallest set.

Then I saw the single light bulbs, and my hopes rose. I got really excited when I discovered that a single red, blue, green, or yellow bulb cost only twenty cents. I knew exactly where I'd put one! Hanging from our porch was a lamp fashioned like a lantern, with bubbly glass on the top and three sides (the bottom glass had broken long ago). In my mind's eye I could see the colored bulb shining out through that glass lantern. That would prove we had Christmas at our house!

As I walked home I schemed how I might get another dime to match the one I had found. My grandma made Christmas wreaths out of running cedar that she collected from the woods. Maybe if I helped her gather evergreens, she would give me a few cents.

Grandma asked for my help on the weekend, as I'd hoped. The prickly, heavily scented cedar caught on my woolen gloves, loosening the yarn as I tore the plants from the ground and stuffed them into the old feedbag. When we had finished, Grandma didn't give me a red cent. My disappointment must have shown, because she asked me if I was feeling okay. I didn't blurt out, "I wanted one measly dime," but I'd wanted to.

A few days later, Uncle Charlie, who was in the army, dropped in to see Mother and to let her know he would be away on duty until March. He gave each of us children a dime to spend as we chose. We jumped and squealed with delight; at the time there were many things you could buy with ten cents.

Just as soon as I could, I went back to the hardware store and bought a single colored light bulb. Back home, I climbed the stepladder and replaced the clear bulb in the porch light with the colored one. After the sun set that afternoon, I switched on the light and, unobserved, slipped outside to inspect the lovely colored light glowing brightly in the darkness. My little chest swelled with pride.

When Daddy came in from work he asked, "Who put the red light on the front porch?"

"I did, Daddy!" I happily confessed. "Doesn't it look Christmasy?"

Tickled pink with myself, I smiled up at him. I was puzzled to see him look at Mother with a funny expression on his face.

The next night a green light glowed from the lantern on our front porch. When I asked my mother what had happened to the red bulb, she told me it had been faulty, so Daddy had replaced it. Red or green, it didn't matter to me. Our house was wearing some holiday spirit, and it looked beautiful.

~Barbara W. Campbell

My Dad, the Pink Lady

My dad and I seldom saw eye to eye when I was growing up in the 1950s. I marched to a different drummer, one he couldn't understand. Oh, he took pride in my accomplishments, but almost daily he would ask my saintly mother, "Why does that boy always have to learn things the hard way?"

It is one of the greatest tragedies of modern life that we never fully appreciate those who have loved us, taught us, and managed somehow to raise us until their counsel is no longer available. Our schedules are just too busy to allow for much reflection until it is often too late to say thank you. The fact that I am not unique in this regard offers little consolation.

I did not fully grasp the enormity of my father's example and counsel until his recent death caused me to carefully consider his many contributions to our family, as well as the principles he stood for throughout his eighty-two years.

Dad was a blue-collar worker who built machines from blueprints. He had a gift for turning absolutely nothing into something useful. He once fashioned a soap-box racer for me out of scrap wood and a metal trash can. It was the envy of the neighborhood, winning our championship race down the infamous Big Hill. Our church's nursery and kindergarten are full of toys he made—some of them fifty years old—and his repair work is evident throughout the building.

My father had a tremendous work ethic. After a forty-one-year career in a machine shop he retired, but only from his paying job. Before his health forced him to stay at home, he had logged in more than 18,000 hours of voluntary service in the local hospital, a record expected to stand for all time. He called himself a "pink lady" and proudly wore his pink volunteer vest and many service pins. Dad's sense of compassion and his good nature endeared him to thousands of patients and their families.

"Mr. H," as all affectionately called him, also had a strong sense of humor. One morning he arrived at the hospital just before daybreak (my father was an early riser). After parking his Lincoln, he began shuffling arthritically toward the hospital door when a security guard called to him.

"Hey, Mr. H, you left your lights on."

Dad stopped, looked back, placed a finger beside his nose, and then pointed sharply at the car. As if on command, the lights turned themselves off.

Dad smiled mischievously. "Thank you," he said to the guard.

My brother and I have often wondered how many days he had tried timing those lights in anticipation of that morning.

One Christmas day my father learned of a woman's vigil at the bedside of her comatose and terminally ill husband. She'd been there for days. Following a somewhat heated discussion in the hospital administration office, he was able to arrange for the woman to use an empty room for a few hours' rest and a shower.

When he came home for Christmas dinner, he told my mother he had just given the most unusual present of his life.

Mom recognized his impish smile and played along. "And what was that, Frank?"

His chest swelled. "I just gave a woman a bath and then put her to bed."

The next day he showed up at the hospital with a big lump on his head. After suffering his peers' meddlesome pestering for a while, he finally uttered matter-of-factly, "My yardstick. My wife. My business."

For a man who had hopped a freight train to a new life during the Depression with only a dime in his pocket and who had later completed only a year of college, my father was both very well read and quite a philosopher. He would always tell me, "Son, you can generally have anything you want from life, but you can't have everything," and "Never give up or give in to adversity." He not only espoused these philosophies, he lived them. Even in the autumn years of his life, while putting up with severe arthritis and asbestosis (lung disorder caused by inhalation of asbestos fibers), he brought warmth, humor, and moral support to countless others.

Late in life, he and Mother moved into an assisted-living apartment at a retirement center. At his funeral I learned he had joined the poetry club there. I found it remarkable that he had regularly stood in front of the group reciting works he had committed to memory sixty-five years earlier. I'm sure Longfellow's "Paul Revere's Ride" had been one of them, as he had recited it so often to us while we were growing up.

Perhaps the advice that grows increasingly meaningful for me with each passing year is my father's famous, "Son, anything you'll ever want to know is written somewhere in a book. So read 'em all." Dad, you were right again, and I trust you wouldn't have minded the fact that I have written a few of them myself. As I finish my fourth novel, I know he is watching and smiling down on me.

My father died on a Friday; we buried him the following Sunday. Only one paper published his obituary on Saturday, but more than 300 people attended the funeral. In the receiving line I kept asking all the hospital employees and volunteers who attended, "Who's running the store? You're all here."

Just days before his death this very wise, devout man had told his wife of sixty years, "You have always made a good home for me. This time I'm going to go ahead and prepare a place for you."

Although Dad and I didn't grow close until his later years, a fact I now lament, I know he passed on satisfied in having seen his two little hellion boys turn into responsible grownups with wonderful children of their own. I know this because not long before the end he told me so.

Thank you, Dad.

~Lynn M. Huffstetler

Holding Your Breath

I t wasn't my first scare as a parent. I muttered those words as we raced to the hospital and several times more, while my husband and I filled out forms, answered endless insurance questions, and rode the elevator to the critical care unit. Like countless mothers of curious, rambunctious children, I'd tended cuts and bruises, sprains and dislocations, even broken bones. Scrapes healed, bones mended. We'd been fortunate, I thought. Lucky.

Yet, entering the ICU, I struggled for composure. Each huff of the respirator brought me closer to panic. My younger son was a sturdy, six-foot college sophomore, known for his easy grin and winning sense of humor, but size and personality could not heal his injuries. Neither could I. The pained expressions and guarded answers from attending physicians told me more than I wanted to know—traumatic brain injury is risky, unpredictable, and at best, life-altering. The prognosis was grim.

It wasn't my first fright, I stubbornly reasoned. I had been here before.

The first time, I'd been on the phone. Doing what? Talking to a neighbor or my sister, maybe fielding a wrong number or unsolicited sales pitch. Whatever the reason, I leaned against the sink, stared out the kitchen window, and absently played with the telephone cord. An odd thud-thud had me glancing over my shoulder.

Eyes wild, Bryan bucked in his highchair. Fingers flexed, legs kicked, but he was eerily silent, and the hard, slender biscuit he'd been sucking had vanished.

I fumbled with the chair's plastic tray, threw it aside, then yanked him up and out. With his back to my chest, I pressed against his sternum, with no result, not like the Red Cross dummies I'd earnestly practiced on, victims who survive heart attacks, strokes, falls from speeding jet planes, because it's only make-believe and there's nothing to lose. I pressed again, a two-finger hold and release. I smacked Bryan's back and turned him upside down, while my own breathing became a shallow pant. I shook and jiggled, as if he were an overstuffed piggybank.

No time for panic. No time to scream for help or race to the local ER. It all fell on me, a frantic mother holding her child's breath in her hands. Life, death; right, wrong. Meanings collapsed into agonizing seconds.

I draped him, face up, over my knee and tilted his chin back. I jabbed my finger in his mouth, past the tiny, white teeth and soft, pink tongue. I poked and clawed. He went limp. Rosy cheeks turned to dull khaki. *For the love of God. Please!*

And just like that, my pinkie hooked the hard stub in his gullet. The teething biscuit flew up and out, food on wings. The most welcomed sound in the universe emerged from my toddler—a raggedy cough, a wondrous yowl.

It was my turn then. I rocked his small, shuddering frame and wailed my own hiccupping sputters.

There'd been other times, too. An allergic reaction to penicillin sent us racing to the hospital—unexpected, because I had been a penicillin poster-child, with enough antibiotic residue in my veins to cure a small, feverish country. Bryan puffed up. His cheeks swelled like an autumn squirrel, and his face turned scarlet. Next time could be fatal, the doctors said.

Close calls, near misses, like the fly-by of a looping comet. Nothing stopped him, not the attack of asthmatic bronchitis at age seven, so severe the symptoms required a three-day hospital stay. He smoked a medicated pipe, and multiple cortisone injections transformed him into a whirling dervish. The congestion cleared, and my husband and I fell into one another's arms, relieved and exhausted.

That particular night, when I'd carted him, feverish and raspy, to the emergency room, he'd whispered against my neck. "Mommy, I think I'm dying."

"Sorry, not allowed," I said. "Moms go first." He sobbed. I shushed and rocked him. "It won't happen for a long time. Pinky-swear."

I didn't realize then that I, too, needed oaths and promises. I should have hired a lawyer, insisted on a binding contract. The reason is simple: A child dying isn't fair. A child dying breaks the rules of nature, that zealous covenant of the heart—children outlive their parents.

All those incidents were simple test-drives for the big moment, this ongoing drama in the ICU, a first look, the grand reveal. Behind curtain number three . . .

No! I'm not ready! Not now, not ever! I wanted to shout.

Oh look, it's a mistake. It's some other mother's son, I wanted to say.

I wanted to laugh nervously, the way you do when you catch yourself in a stumble. "A close call," you might say, still convinced you're a special case, somehow immune to senseless harm and injury, and even more naively, believing luck and good intentions will protect your loved ones.

Standing in the critical-care cubicle, I quickly realized that Bryan's condition was beyond promises, luck, and wishful thinking. Whatever preparatory experience I thought I'd had vanished in a heartbeat. An array of machines blinked and beeped. The respirator heaved its rhythmic whoosh. A bedside, chest-tube pump gurgled like a fish aquarium.

Bryan's face and neck were grotesquely swollen. His right cheek was raw, the skin abraded, weeping yellow. His eyelids bulged, and the flesh looked pounded, pummeled to a midnight blue.

I touched his shoulder and stroked his hair. I patted his cheek, then ran my hands along the length of him, the way you examine a newborn. Far worse were the injuries I could not see. Bryan's skin was clammy, and his feet were arched as if he were ready to dance on point. I would find out later that this stiff, unnatural positioning, known as "posturing," was a telling symptom of brain trauma.

Despite all the touching, Bryan lay perfectly still. I patted the tattoo on his upper left arm, a tribal bracelet I'd complained about months earlier. "Wrong place, wrong tribe. . . . Self-indulgent, body graffiti," I'd said when he came home and declared it was his decision, his body. "Would you deface a church, a holy shrine?" I'd replied, indignantly.

How stupid and self-righteous I'd been. I would have swapped these injuries for a dozen tattoos—snakes and vines and provocative women that gyrate with a simple flex of muscle. I would have gladly inked my own indelible message: Don't you dare die.

Stretched naked and vulnerable on the hospital bed, Bryan looked smaller, shorter than I remembered, as if inches had been lopped off during the time he'd stood atop a fraternity house roof, probably laughing riotously, and the time he'd fallen, a thirty-foot drop. Had he realized what was happening? Once he'd lost his footing and jack-knifed through the paper-sharp air, did he think, *This is it, the obliterating end?* Had he been terrified, seen his life play out, a short, disappointing film? I would torture myself for days with useless questions.

I leaned in and whispered, "I'm holding your breath, Bryan. I have it right here in my hands."

No sign he heard me.

A nurse patted my shoulder. "Time to go," she said. Time for surgery and kisses and tearful good-byes. All the time in the world but never enough when you really need it.

Equipment was adjusted for transport, and two burly attendants rolled Bryan into the hallway. A white sheet, covering him from neck to toe, fluttered as they rolled down the corridor on wobbly wheels. John and I shuffled behind, the stunned witnesses. With a bump and jiggle, the gurney disappeared onto a waiting elevator. Steel doors closed with a hiss.

We returned to the ICU cubicle, but there was nothing of Bryan there. While we waited, time settled in like a dense fog. The world shifted into slow motion, and the universe's grand cosmic expansion came to a shuddering halt.

From the hospital's fifth floor, I watched automobiles chug along the street and parking lot. Pedestrians jogged in place at the crosswalk, hugged themselves or clapped their hands. Other passersby tilted their heads and laughed. Swirls of breath streamed out, long and white. *Didn't they know?* I wanted to scream. *Couldn't they see the world had tilted and turned upside down?*

I held my son's breath once. His life had ebbed and surged in my hands.

Now, I recited childhood prayers, pleading for better hands, bigger and stronger, so his unfinished life wouldn't slip through my fingers. John and I leaned into one another. We held on the best we knew how.

It was only later, after witnessing Bryan's agonizing recovery, that I realized my husband and I had tumbled, too, free-fallen through a vast, dark space. There were long days and longer nights to come. I would learn the rehab rule for traumatic brain injury—three steps forward, two steps back. An exhausting dance. But I would also relearn the value of family, friends, and neighbors. My sister and best friend braved a harrowing, six-hour road trip in a blizzard to join us at the hospital. Neighbors I barely knew cooked and delivered months of homemade meals. My in-laws dropped their own lives, moved into our home, and took charge of routine matters— unpaid bills, house maintenance, and our abandoned kennel-shy dog.

It wasn't my first scare as a parent, but I would remember it differently. Eight years ago, we relied on family and friends but also countless strangers—doctors, nurses, and tireless therapists—to do what my husband and I could not do alone: save our son's life. There were other people I never met who helped put Bryan back together again. An anonymous caller dialed 911 and then, audibly shaken, alerted us of the accident. The emergency squad responded in less than three minutes and resuscitated Bryan at the scene. The ER staff, who had little confidence in our son's long-term survival, worked feverishly to stabilize him.

But there was more.

Bryan fought back with astonishing ferocity. I'd like to think he inherited my stubborn gene. He surpassed the sobering predictions of his physicians and caretakers. He learned to crawl, then walk, then gradually resume his life, adjusting to frustrating memory lapses, a chronic weakness on his left side, and the raw reality that young or old, we are fragile, finite creatures. He has since graduated college, carved out a career and will soon be married.

I have to believe our lives are configured and laced together in ways I cannot know or imagine. And that's okay, the not knowing. It's enough, I think, to acknowledge what we don't know, to pay homage to generous, unseen interventions, and to honor the loyalty and love of family and friends.

This wasn't my first scare as a parent, but it is the event against which all others are measured: the night my son, my husband, and I fell from a great height, were held for a single, quivering moment, and then like bewildered but humbled children returned safely to the ground.

~Margaret A. Frey

Guiding Lights

Toña needed a break. So did her two best friends, Mary and Vicky. Each of the young women was going through her individual "rough patch," and all felt emotionally, physically, and spiritually spent. The three friends reasoned that by pooling their limited financial resources, they would be able to afford a weekend away together at some peaceful place within a reasonable driving distance from Los Angeles, but far from its congestion. They called around and were thrilled to find an inexpensive cabin in the San Bernardino Mountains that was available the following weekend. They paid the deposit and finalized the plans for their road trip.

They decided to take Vicky's car, a sleek, black, late-model Toyota Corolla with a five-speed standard transmission. Because Vicky didn't like driving long distances and Mary didn't like driving curvy roads,

Toña took the wheel on the late Friday afternoon of their departure. They were all glad to get away and excited about the upcoming weekend. They had no particular plans for what they would do once they got there, other than to relax and enjoy themselves. The drive up to Big Bear Lake was smooth and fun, and time passed quickly as the three friends chatted away, sang along to their favorite tapes on the stereo, and reminisced about childhood camping experiences in the mountains.

The weekend was just what each of them needed. They spent time together in easy companionship, and gave each other the space to do whatever each wanted or needed to do. Mary went to the lake early Saturday morning and sat for a long spell in solitude. There among the pines, she communed with nature and asked God for direction, as she was at a turning point in her life. Toña went for a hike and found a large tree to climb; she sat high in the branches reading and thinking. Vicky stayed in the cabin, curled up with a good book.

Feeling refreshed and relaxed, they were on the road by noon on Sunday, with a picnic basket packed with lunch and high hopes for a fun trip home. They impulsively stopped at Santa's Village, the source of many joyous childhood memories. Though their adult eyes took note of the white paint streaked with glitter, their little-girl hearts told them it was snow on the rooftops. With joyful abandon, the three friends rode the sleigh ride and the Ferris wheel, drank hot chocolate, and ate rock candy and caramel apples (not caring if it spoiled their appetites).

When they finally left the amusement park, they continued on to Arrowhead Lake, where they stopped to eat their picnic lunch, which they had stored in the trunk of the car. Afterward, they picked up some drinks at a fast-food drive-through and set out for home. Mary and Vicky sipped their sodas, while Toña drank iced tea. She didn't mention to her companions that her tea tasted funny or that her stomach felt queasy.

Mary suggested that they take a detour through the Redlands so that she could show her friends Jenk's Lake, which she'd told them about enjoying as a child on the way up. Vicky said it sounded fun, and despite the rumblings in her tummy, Toña had no objections.

It was late afternoon by the time they found Jenk's Lake, which turned out to be as remote, picturesque, and serene as Mary had claimed. It was the off-season, so they had the whole lake and campgrounds to themselves. They parked the car in the empty parking lot and strolled down to the shore. Mary led her friends on a walk from one end of the lake to the other, recounting tales of her adventures there as a young camper. They lingered, enjoying the sunset in that peaceful, beautiful place. Finally, with dusk approaching, they reluctantly returned to the car.

Both Vicky and Mary had poor night vision, so Toña took the driver's seat again, saying nothing to her friends about her upset stomach. She started the engine and turned on the lights, but she couldn't see any light beaming from the headlamps. The other girls hopped out of the car, Vicky to check the lights in the front, Mary the back. They had parking lights, but no headlights or taillights. Toña pressed the brake pedal, and Mary gave the thumbs up; at least those worked.

They did everything they knew to do: checked fuses, checked for loose wires and faulty connections, tapped on housings, turned the lights on and off. Nothing worked. There were no pay phones at the remote spot, and they had no cell phone. They thought briefly of spending the night in the unlit parking lot but quickly realized that that wasn't a good plan. Deciding that their only option was to try and get down the mountain before the dusk turned to night, they got back on the road.

Mary and Vicky chatted and sang songs, while Toña concentrated all her efforts on navigating without headlights the narrow, curvy mountain road she'd never driven before. As the sick feeling in her stomach turned to painful cramps, Toña sent up silent prayers that she could keep from throwing up and keep the car on the road. Gritting her teeth, she focused intently on the unlit, two-lane road, driving as fast as she safely could in the deepening darkness.

Total blackness descended upon them long before they'd wound their way through the dark pine forest and down the mountain. Mary and Vicky grew silent, giving Toña the quiet they knew she needed to concentrate.

Toña slowed to 15 miles per hour, a necessary but dangerous maneuver. A black car with no taillights creeping along a dark mountain road on a moonless night at less than half the speed limit was a slow-moving target for any vehicle blasting down the mountain behind them. The three friends all knew that there was a strong possibility that they could be rear-ended and perhaps knocked off the road and over the side of the mountain by a car whose driver didn't see them until it was too late. With only the parking lights to illuminate the road, however, it was impossible to drive safely at a higher speed.

Suddenly, they noticed headlights far behind them, and that the vehicle was fast approaching. Toña tapped the brake pedal, hoping the driver would understand her signal to slow down, hoping that the brake lights still worked. She was gratified to see the red glow in the rear-view mirror, assuring her they did work. But the vehicle continued to bear down on them. The three friends held their breath as Toña pumped the brake frantically and they all exhaled deeply when the other car finally slowed down. The driver expressed his unhappiness by honking and flashing his lights. When they finally reached a short stretch of straight road, he passed, shouting and cursing at them to turn on their lights.

Another car came up behind them. Again, Toña tapped the brakes to alert the other driver to the danger. Again, the driver honked and flashed his lights, then passed and yelled at them. A third car appeared, and a similar scene played itself out. Each time, Mary, Vicky, and Toña sighed with relief and sent up another silent prayer of thanks and for help.

Then a fourth vehicle approached from behind. That driver drew up close to the back fender of their car, slowed to match Toña's speed, and then just hovered there. The girls were confused and nervous. What was going on?

The driver turned on his high beams. The bright lights shone into the interior rear-view mirror of the Toyota, nearly blinding and greatly annoying Toña. Then she noticed that the high beams from the other vehicle lit up the road in front of her, and she realized the other driver was deliberately lighting their way. She let out a whoop and turned the mirror at an angle to cut the reflection.

Mary and Vicky cried out with joy.

"He's a guardian angel sent to rescue us!" Mary said.

"Just keep following us, fella!" Vicky said.

Toña gradually increased her speed as much as she could, traveling 20 to 25 miles per hour as visibility allowed. All the while, the vehicle with the guiding lights kept a consistent distance behind her. For almost an hour, they were guided by the lights of the other vehicle down the twisting mountain road. Mary and Vicky thought it was a car; Toña insisted it was a truck.

As they came around the last bend in the road and started descending into the city lights below, Toña suggested that they pull over at the first stop sign or traffic light to thank the driver of the other vehicle. Her friends agreed.

When they reached the stop sign, Toña quickly pulled over, and the three friends got out, but there was no car or truck behind them. In fact, there were no other vehicles in sight, and the only sound they heard was the low purr of the Toyota's engine. The guiding lights had been behind them when they'd pulled up to the stop sign, and they had passed no side streets or driveways or pull-outs onto which the other driver might have suddenly turned.

Stunned, the three friends piled wordlessly back into the car and headed toward a restaurant a short distance ahead.

"Well," Toña finally said. "I guess that really was a guardian angel, because there wasn't anybody else back there but us."

They entered the restaurant, and while Mary and Vicky slid into a booth and ordered dinner, Toña raced to the bathroom and became violently ill from the food poisoning she'd contracted—either from the lunch that had been stored in the trunk of the car or the iced tea that had tasted strange to her.

Vicky called the auto club, and the three friends spent the night in a motel. The next morning the local mechanic could find nothing wrong with the car's lights. Later, Vicky's regular mechanic finally found and repaired a short in the electrical system.

Mary, Toña, and Vicky each returned from the weekend they had spent together feeling closer to one another and to their individual spiritual truths—certain in the knowledge that no matter how dark the night, a guiding light would always be available to illuminate the road ahead.

~*Toña Morales-Calkins*

The Blue Washcloth

The comforting, musical sloshing and tinkling of the water, the only sounds in the otherwise quiet house, served to calm the air. The battle was over; a compromise had been struck, and the bath had been undertaken, albeit tentatively. At first, she had thought that he was only being stubborn and rude in his refusal to take a shower. Didn't getting cleaned up always make a person feel better? Didn't he realize how offensive his odor was? She'd even offered to do all the work, telling him that all he had to do was sit on the little bath stool. Still he'd refused.

He had accused her of being bitchy and controlling. Didn't she understand how weak he had become, how devastated by disease and pain? Of course, he smelled of death; he was dying.

The dog sensed it, too, and seemed confused by

this living/dying impersonator of her former master. From sleeping at the side of the hospital bed in the front room, the dog had relocated to the foot of it, then across near the doorway, and now only kept a watchful eye from the next room.

After his harsh rebuke in response to her pleading, she had finally just asked him, "Why?"

And he, perhaps finally seeing that she was only desperate to help him, answered, defeat in his voice, "I just can't."

Her eyes opened wide and filled with tears. *My God, the man can't even sit in a bath.*

He kept doing this to her. He was so damnably stoic, hiding the truth so that she was always days behind in grasping the extent of his misery. He was slipping away so fast. So fast. There seemed to be no time to adapt to one devastating piece of news before the next one hit.

She asked, "Would you like me to give you a sponge bath here in the bed?"

The connection had been made at last. His eyes were moist now, too. "You would do that?"

"Of course."

And knowing that he hated for her to see him so emotional, that he loathed being seen as weak, she turned away and rose to make the preparations. The round table near the bed, so laden with medications and supplies, was cleared; a basin of warm water, soap, a towel, and washcloth brought. She chose the blue washcloth—blue was his favorite color. How sad that his life had narrowed to such a small sliver of experience that the color of a washcloth could take on such importance. Her efforts to do something—anything—to please him had been forced to shrink down to fit into that sliver. He probably wouldn't notice the color of the washcloth, but if he did . . . well, it should be blue.

She swished the washcloth around in the warm water, then took it up and wrung it out, the water tinkling back into the basin. No words were spoken, because no words were necessary for some time. The physical contact, the warmth of the water, the soothing repetitive strokes of the cloth were sufficient.

Not like her, this quiet. She would usually be making some conversation, staving off any embarrassment or discomfort with small talk. But not now.

He did seem embarrassed and uncomfortable, but little by little, as the perspiration and soil were washed away, so, too, was his unease, and she noticed that he had closed his eyes and wore an expression of peace. Not like him, this peace.

The blue cloth was once more dipped, swished, and wrung out. She washed his neck, puffy and hard along the sides where the tumors had won. As the water trickled down her wrists, so, too, did the memories of the stories he had once told her rise to the surface of her mind. She recalled what an unhappy childhood he had had. That his father had died before he'd even known his wife was pregnant. That he had always felt he was a hardship for his only, reluctant, parent. A burden.

He had said, "I love watching you nurture your children. I never had that, you know; I don't recall ever having been rocked or held or sung to. On a good day, I was tolerated."

She remembered him telling of how, one time as a small boy, he had received a deep cut on his foot and there had been no show of concern or attempt to comfort him. Instead, his caretaker had acted as if it were an inconvenience to have to interrupt her routine to bandage him.

Again and again, the blue washcloth was rinsed in the basin and wrung out. The pleasant sound of the dripping water filled the room as she held up his arm to wash it. New lumpy tumors filled the area between his armpit and breast. The cancer was winning—had won; there was no need to mention the discovery of the new tumors or to call the doctor. They had reached the end of the fight.

From top to bottom, she bathed him. His eyes were closed, but hers suddenly opened. Revelation flooded in, overwhelming her, causing her almost to swoon. She looked at him with profound understanding. Was overcome by a sense of reverence. She considered carefully, prayerfully.

"Oh, I see," she said simply, rinsing out the washcloth yet again.

"See what?" he asked, not opening his eyes.

"I see. God has shown me that his love is too awesome for words."

"Oh it is, is it?" The same reluctant tolerance for her spiritual references.

"Yes. He loves you so very much he has allowed you to have lung cancer."

"Lucky me." The old sarcasm had not diminished along with the wasting away of his body.

"No, really." She was bursting to help him share in the monumental revelation she had just experienced. "I think when it's your time, it's your time. You could have been hit by a truck or had a sudden heart attack. But God has put you in a position where you must receive what you need for your soul.

"Here you are, being stroked and petted for the first time in your life. You were never open to being cared for in this way before, because you had never experienced it as a child. Look at how relaxed you are now. Cancer has taken away those walls you've had up all this time."

His eyes were closed tight, but that could not keep the stream of tears from slipping silently down his cheeks.

"And he loves you so much, he gave me to you," she continued, gently, assuredly. "I am a nurturer. That's what I do. I can't do anything about the disease, but perhaps I can help heal your heart. And I want you to know that I don't mind this a bit. I am not embarrassed or resentful or offended or uncomfortable at all about doing this. You are my husband. You need a bath. It is that simple."

She dipped the blue washcloth and wrung it out and reached toward him again. This time, he intercepted her ministering hands. Clutched them with the old strength and drew her dripping fingers to his lips, where the bath water mingled with his tears. He kissed her hands and said only, softly, "Thank you."

Directing his gaze upward, he said it again—his first prayer: "Thank you."

~*Diane M. Vogel*

A Special Day

"Come on, Anthony. This is your special day! We need to go now."

"Okay, Mom," the four-year-old boy shouted as he ran from the sparsely furnished living room into the kitchen.

"Oh, Anthony!" she exclaimed, looking down at his shoes. As usual, they were on the wrong feet. "We're going to miss the streetcar."

Still, she smiled as she undid his shoes, placed them on the correct feet, and carefully tied the laces. "How are your feet, sweetie?"

"Okey-dokey."

Anthony lived with his parents and two older sisters in a small apartment in a converted army barracks on the "down" side of Toronto. It was all they could afford. His dad was sick and rarely worked, and his mom earned a meager living as the "superintendent" of the tenement where they lived. Her job duties included cleaning the common toilets and washing all the floors. She was a humble, hard-working woman who was fiercely protective of her children and totally committed to her ailing husband. Anthony never heard her complain, and she always had a hug and a smile for her family.

Anthony's family had salvaged many of their belongings from the army dump behind their building. The army was always throwing away surplus material that was still usable. The soldiers on dump duty were ordered to destroy the discards so as to prevent civilians from scavenging and reusing them. Still, some of the soldiers recognized the needs of the poor and would place still-useful articles in a certain place, knowing they would find grateful homes.

The tenement where Anthony's family lived had no yard or playground. Sometimes Anthony played in the dump. Sometimes he snuck through the fence and onto the artillery range next door. He'd stare deep into the dark holes left by the mortar impacts, catch pollywogs in those craters, or just lay on his back in the cool grass and stare at the clouds.

When Anthony was three years old, his mother had taken him to a doctor who had said he had malformed feet and needed specially constructed shoes. The doctor had advised that Anthony be fitted for the shoes before he got much bigger. He had said that they would aid in his walking and perhaps even correct the problem. As the weeks and months passed and there never seemed to be enough money for the orthopedic shoes, Anthony's mother began to worry.

Finally, she decided that, for Anthony's sake, they couldn't afford to wait any longer. One day, while his two sisters were at school and his dad slept, Anthony and his mom headed for the orthopedic shoe shop in the city.

Anthony was excited to be going downtown on the streetcar—and when Anthony was excited, he asked questions. In fact, Anthony always had a lot of questions, usually asked in rapid-fire succession.

"Can we sit up front? Will I be able to see the conductor?"

"Yes, honey, if there's a seat. Yes, we will."

As they walked the five blocks to the streetcar hand-in-hand, Anthony fired off questions nonstop.

"Can hot water put out a fire?"

"Why do bees sting?"

"What color is water at night?"

"My goodness," his mother said, laughing. "Do you ever run out of questions?"

The trolley car arrived, and Anthony lobbed his questions at the conductor.

"Hey, mister conductor, how fast will the streetcar go?"

"How come you don't have to steer?"

"Why do you ring that bell?"

The driver looked over and raised his eyebrows at Anthony's mom, who could only chuckle and shrug her shoulders.

They soon arrived downtown and walked a short distance to the shop. His mother had called beforehand to make an appointment to have Anthony measured and fitted for the new shoes.

"Hey, what's that?" Anthony started questioning the craftsman. "Are you going to measure my feet? Will it hurt?"

"Now, Anthony, let the nice man do what he has to. He's going to help make your feet all better."

"You bet we are," he said, winking at Anthony.

During the next half-hour, Anthony asked fifty or so questions, each of which the shoemaker patiently fielded. When the shoemaker was finished with the measurements, he gave the little boy a lollipop and his mom the estimate of what it would cost to build Anthony's corrective footwear: $55.

Anthony's mother looked surprised and then upset. She knew that there was no possible way she could come up with anything close to that amount. She quietly thanked the shoemaker for his time and told him she would have to think about it. Heartbroken, she left the shop with Anthony, still sucking on his lollipop, in tow.

"C'mon, Tony," she said, forcing a smile to hide her disappointment. "Let's go get a hot dog."

"Oh boy!"

After they had shared a hot dog and a soda, Anthony and his mother took the trolley back to their neighborhood. Hand-in-hand, they walked the same five-block stretch of deserted sidewalk that earlier had held so much promise.

"What is that?" Anthony's mom asked, as they reached the front stoop of their building.

There, beside the doorway, was a small box carefully wrapped in brown paper and tied with a string. It looked almost like a present but without the colorful paper.

There was no one around, so Anthony's mother picked up the box and jiggled it, like a child might before opening a Christmas present. They heard only indistinguishable muffled thuds from within the box.

"I wonder what it is and whom it belongs to," she said, more to herself than to Anthony. "Should we open it and try to find out?"

"Yes! Open it! Open it!"

She stretched the string around first one corner, then another. The paper that had been folded around it came away easily. She lifted the lid and her hand flew to her mouth.

"Oh my. Oh my, Anthony!"

Then she tilted the box so he could see. It contained a pair of the special, made-to-order shoes, just like the ones he'd tried on in the shop. And they fit his measurements exactly.

As Anthony's mother had promised, it had turned out to be a special day indeed.

~Anthony Merlocco

Sing Your Song

My aunt once had a canary who loved to sing along with her vacuum cleaner. For some reason, the sound of its motor filled the bird's heart with musical inspiration, and he would respond with counter-melodies that trilled high above its roar.

The canary demonstrated the extent of his dedication to his art one unforgettable day when my aunt decided to clean her draperies. As she hauled out the vacuum cleaner and attached the extension hose, the bird's delight at the prospect of making music with his favorite accompaniment was actually visible. My aunt turned on the machine, and the little bird responded with an aria seemingly inspired by the angels.

My aunt eventually became so involved in her task that she didn't notice that her pet warbler had emerged from his cage and had flown to the top of the cornice. As she lifted the vacuum wand to get into the drapery folds, she suddenly saw a flash of yellow disappear down the tube.

Horrified, she immediately switched off the machine, certain that her poor bird had, indeed, joined the angels. Then she paused, cocking her ear closer to the vacuum cleaner—and heard the unmistakable sound of her bird's muffled song, emanating from within.

"Keep singing, darling!" called my aunt. "Mama will save you!"

She quickly unzipped the bag, and the bird's voice burst forth sweet and strong. Burrowing her hand deep into the dirt and dust bunnies, she at last cleared a pathway through which her pet could escape.

The bird shot out from the bag like a bullet and landed on the coffee table: singing. With a new sense of awe and respect, my aunt gazed at her pet as he continued with his symphony—despite the fact that his body had been stripped of all of its feathers.

When I picture that little bird's perseverance in proclaiming his *joie de vivre* to the world, I wonder what the world would be like if the human race could equal such dedication. What if we, like my aunt's canary, refused to let anything keep us from singing our own glorious song, so to speak?

Whenever I think of that joyous little bird,

I resolve to sing my own song loudly and clearly, uninhibited by whatever obstacles might threaten to silence me. It is, after all, my gift to myself and to the world.

~Lynn Ruth Miller

More Precious Than Gold

The kids return to school in the fall and before long, it happens: kitchen counters everywhere start sinking like the Titanic under the weight of the massive paper load sent home from class each day. At least, that's what happens at my house.

This is a pile of papers that, no matter which strategies I deploy to squelch it, I cannot make go away. I've tried moving it elsewhere, but the pile always seems to magnetize itself back to that same roosting spot on my counter. I've also tried tossing the papers, burning them, shredding them, and turning them into something more useful (Thanksgiving stuffing). But when the pile senses its life is threatened, it activates its regenerative instinct and instantly swells to quadruple its size.

I have married, given birth four times, signed my name to a mortgage, and had my eyebrows hot waxed. None of that strikes the same terror in my heart as seeing my little darlings' bulging backpacks come through the door after school. Unloading fist-fuls of papers, they add them to the stack. The larger the stack, the smaller my self-esteem.

I cannot—can*not*—keep track of the deluge of notes concerning supplies to be purchased, scout registrations, book orders due, PTO meetings, fund-raisers, bus-schedule changes, parent volunteering, school sweatshirts to buy, class picture money to send in, snack day sign-ups, holiday party–planning meet-ings to attend, and who knows what else because no one in this house has managed to get to the piece of paper holding the secrets to all these must-dos.

The papers also remind me that I am supposed to prepare each of my four children for their weekly spelling tests; quiz them on their math facts; help them study for their upcoming science, history, or geography tests; edit their English papers; review their journals; check and sign their homework; fur-ther enhance their learning by doing suggested "fun" home activities during my "spare" time; listen to them read every night—and clone myself into four equal parts. That's the only possible way to get all this stuff done.

I fail horribly, unable to keep pace with all the fliers and notices that the school cranks out on the paper machine; I feel like Lucy and Ethel trying to keep up with the speeding chocolate on the assembly line. I have a calendar I try to write these things down on, but by the time I actually get around to sorting through the papers, I sometimes find I'm off by several years.

I work through the pile and find my daughter's spelling test from three weeks ago, with half the words marked wrong. Thirteen inches under that, I find that week's spelling list, which I was supposed to go over with her four weeks ago.

I redeem myself by quizzing my other daughter on her shapes.

"That's not *my* homework," she says, insulted.

"It has your teacher's name on it," I insist.

"That was my *preschool* teacher!" she, now a sixth grader, points out.

These papers mock my mothering, making me feel like a miserable failure. I'm sure my children wouldn't argue the fact. After all, I've sent these kids to school with permission slips for field trips they've already taken.

They are no doubt tired of being the only kids in their class who are singled out daily to receive reminder notes concerning some paper I've forgotten to respond to, send in, or sign. (How helpful to cure a fire with more fire.) I can only imagine how quickly they will dissociate themselves from me ("I've never seen that woman before in my life!") when again this year I arrive for the school Valentine's party dressed in my Halloween costume.

Yesterday, I stood hip-deep in the pile, cursing the invention of paper and ink as I slogged through a thick stack of my third-grade son's weekly work that had been stapled together for me to review and sign. Burrowing 1,795 papers into the stack, I stumbled upon an assignment that caught my eye.

On the top was printed: "Something that is as precious as gold to me is _____," with the blank to be filled in by the student.

My son had written, "My mom is as precious as gold to me, because I love her." It was illustrated with a crayoned heart containing two cartoon figures with matching hairdos who were hugging and smiling.

Like I was saying, I just adore that glorious stack of papers on my kitchen counter.

~Denise Wahl

The Windfall

My parents were born at the turn of the century and found themselves caught in the Great Depression with four mouths to feed. My father, Joe, worked part-time in the oil fields, and my mother, Della, cooked for the roustabouts who lived in the bunkhouse.

As the Depression eased, a long dry spell parched the earth, cracking the soil and turning it white. Emboldened by hunger, jack rabbits nibbled every last leaf from shrubs. Hot winds howled. Dust blew in the cracks, and Della hung damp sheets over doors and windows. Water was precious, but she used what was left from rinsing dishes to keep her lilac bush alive. Then the grasshoppers came and chewed it down to a nub. Furious, she beat at them with a towel, but when she saw the futility of it, she buried her face in her apron and wept.

To cheer her, Joe took Della to Reno to play slots and Keno. It was the last of their money, but such was their desperation that they were willing to gamble it.

No sooner had they arrived than Della settled herself in the soft chairs of the Keno parlor and began to mark tickets. Seven of her eight spots showed up on her first ticket . . . $1,800! It was almost as much money as Joe earned in one year.

She stuffed the thick piles—ninety $20 bills—in her black patent leather handbag. Clutching it to her breast, she found Joe near the quarter machines.

"Joe," she gasped, "I've won eighteen-hundred dollars!"

"You what? Oh, Della, be careful. Don't talk about it. We could be robbed!"

"I've got to go to the bathroom, quick! Here, take my purse."

"I can't hold that thing. Take it with you."

Laying the purse at the back of the toilet, Della tried to quiet her thumping heart. When she could stand without fainting, she washed her hands and left the bathroom.

Joe paced near the lady's room door. "Are you okay? You look pale."

"Well, I am now, but I thought I was going to faint before I could get set down."

"Well, let's go. I want to head home before dark. And we've got to find a way to hide that money. Your purse . . . where's your purse?"

"I don't know. I thought I gave it to you."

"I wouldn't take it. You took it in the bathroom with you. Remember?"

"Oh, my stars! I think I left it at the back of the stall."

He grasped her arm and turned her around. "Which bathroom?"

"I think it was right over here."

Disoriented, they searched and finally found the bathroom. She offered a quick prayer that the purse, still holding her winnings, would be where she'd left it. She chose a stall and looked in. There was the black bag.

"Did you look and see? Is the money still in it?"

"Let's get to the car first."

They huddled in the front seat of the Ford and opened the bag.

"It's here! What a miracle!"

"Well, who knows where you'll leave that purse next! Let me have it."

Joe grabbed a half-empty Kleenex box from the car and carefully layered the bills between folds of the tissues. *The perfect hiding place,* he thought. "If we get stopped by thieves, they'll never think to look in here." He put the box in the trunk, and they started home with their fortune.

They arrived the next day in the midst of a dust storm. Blowing sand scoured the black paint from the fenders of the Ford. They struggled to the back of the car, and Joe opened the trunk. "You get the box of tissues," he shouted.

Holding her hat with one hand and gripping her handbag under her arm, Della reached for the box. Suddenly, the gale's force pulled tissues out of the box and sent them sailing across the desert.

Gasping, Della dropped her bag and let go of her hat and clutched the box to her, but the wind had already emptied it. Every last Kleenex and all ninety bills were gone.

Dejected and exhausted beyond tears, they went into the darkened house. Silently, they shook the sand from their clothing, washed the dust from their hands and faces, and went to bed. Joe held Della tenderly and whispered, "It's okay. We'll find the money when the wind dies."

They woke to a calm morning. As soon as the rising sun turned the sagebrush pink, they went out to look for money, hoping some had caught on bushes or wooden derricks. They searched until it was time for Joe to go to work but found only three bills. They could hardly speak.

Joe walked to the bunkhouse, where he told the men the story of the flying money. "Gone with the wind," he said, "gone with the wind!"

Everyone offered help. "God knows a man needs every cent he can get his hands on."

By the time a month passed, the men had found most of the twenties. Each time, the finder, often in oily overalls, walked into the kitchen, hand outstretched, wearing a big grin on his face. Always, my parents offered half in return. Usually, it was turned away with thanks. "It was a pleasure. The day goes fast walking through sagebrush like a kid on a treasure hunt."

Joe and Della hugged and danced around the kitchen. "Let's give a barn dance," they said. "Maybe it's the only way they'll let us thank them."

Their windfall, lost and found, then lost again, had been returned by the goodness of others. From that day forward, they knew where their real riches lay—in the hearts of their friends. They were never anything but rich.

~Audrey Yanes

The Saint of
Subsidized Housing

The first time I met Hector Juarez he told me he was Superman. I told him I didn't believe him.

I was the police officer sent to arrest the person causing the disturbance in the courtyard of the low-income housing project. That person was Hector.

"I-am-Superman!" he shouted again, raising his short arms and posing as if in a bodybuilding competition. I guessed Hector stood 5 feet 4 inches and weighed no more than 110 pounds fully clothed. Nevertheless, I was fearful. I'd detected the odor of ether on his clothing, which usually indicated that the person had taken the violence-inducing hallucinogenic drug PCP. I'd seen guys smaller than Hector do serious bodily harm to policemen twice their size while under the influence of PCP.

"Why don't you just turn around and put your hands up against the side of the building so nobody gets hurt," I suggested. I watched him closely, trying to gauge his potential for violence. When he bent down, picked up a piece of metal pipe, and growled, I knew things were about to turn ugly.

I unsnapped my holster and lifted my pistol, lining the sights up with Hector's chest. He growled more viciously and began to move toward me.

"Stop!" A woman screamed and ran between us. Crying hysterically, she threw her arms around Hector's neck and tried to pull him away. With the narcotic pulsing through his nervous system, Hector was easily able to push the woman aside, knocking her to the ground. He refocused his attention on me. I pulled back the hammer of my automatic.

Shaken but undeterred, the woman knelt down between Hector and me and started to pray.

"Oh God, please take away the evil that is here," she begged. "Stop the power of the drug inside my husband, Hector. Stop the power of fear and hostility in this police officer. Please, Lord, stop it now."

Never before in my police career had I seen anything like this, nor have I since. Apparently, neither had Hector. It instantly disarmed both of us, figuratively and literally. Hector let the pipe drop to the pavement, and I reholstered my gun. Looking skyward, his wife whispered, "Thank you." Then she stood and took hold of Hector's now docile hand.

"God will repay you for your kindness in letting Hector go home with me, Officer," she said, edging her husband toward some distant hallway.

Whoa, hold on there, I thought. I hadn't said anything about letting him just walk away, but I felt powerless to do anything but smile at Hector's unusual wife and wish them good night.

More than a year later I was dispatched to another housing project to check on an individual who matched the description of an escaped mental patient. Two women informed me that the man I was looking for was standing at the center of the local basketball court, screaming. I walked across a vacant lot to the basketball court and saw two things that made me very uncomfortable: a large man standing at center court shouting something about space people, and six members of one of the most violent gangs in the city.

I radioed my situation to a dispatcher, who informed me that all backup units were busy and to handle the situation as best I could until backup was available. I figured the gang members had been waiting for a police offer to respond to the psychotic man, and when that opportunity arose, planned to attack. Unfortunately, I was right.

Knowing the escaped mental patient was considered violent, I approached him cautiously, speaking in gentle tones and avoiding sudden movements. This strategy worked until I was within 10 feet of the man, when he suddenly charged me with the power and ferociousness of a raging bull. Though I managed to side-step most of the impact, I still ended up face down on top of the struggling man. As I worked to gain control of his flailing arms and legs, I was only partially aware that the gang members had come onto the court and had formed a circle around us. Once I had the mental patient more or less restrained, I glanced up at the gang and knew I was in serious danger. Unable to let go of the still highly agitated patient, I could do nothing to protect my exposed back from the gang. With no other alternative available, I reached for my gun.

It was gone.

Realizing it had been knocked out of my holster when I fell to the pavement, I looked around for it frantically and saw that it was in the hand of one of the gang members—and that it was pointed directly at me. I thought about my wife and three kids, what it would be like for them without me, and what it would feel like to be shot with my own gun. I looked up at the gang member holding my gun, waiting for the flash of the muzzle and resulting pain, but he was distracted by something at the far end of the basketball court.

Still struggling to keep the mental patient from escaping, I turned my head to see what had drawn their attention. Walking toward us were Hector and ten of what must have been his biggest friends.

Wordlessly, Hector and his friends pushed through the circle of gang members and formed another, tighter, circle around the psychotic man and me.

"What you doing?" Hector asked, obviously enjoying my predicament.

"Trying to get this man to my cruiser."

"Where's your gun, man? Last time we met, you had a gun."

"It fell out when this guy knocked me down," I said, breathing so hard I could scarcely speak. I nodded toward the guy holding my gun and gasped, "He has it."

Hector turned to look at the gang member and then back to me.

"They don't like you or me, but they like you less. They want to hurt you real bad," he said in a low voice. "I can't fight them to help a cop. They don't want to take on my friends. See what I'm saying?"

Still struggling with the mental patient, I just looked at Hector, fearing I might pass out at any moment.

"Me and my friends are going to just stand here

and watch a police officer do his job. Going to watch all the way to the car. See what I'm saying?"

I did.

Though I was exhausted from the wrestling match, so was the patient. I eventually handcuffed him, helped him to his feet, and led him toward my cruiser.

It certainly was a strange sight: a lone police officer and a man screaming about space aliens, surrounded by two concentric circles of rival gangs, each with differing motives, all moving across the basketball court.

True to his word, Hector and his friends encircled me with their protection across the court and the vacant lot, parting only slightly when we reached the patrol car. As I tucked the now subdued mental patient into the back seat, an anonymous hand dropped my gun onto the front seat.

"Thanks," I said, my voice thick with emotion.

"Payback," Hector said, grinning.

I started the car and backed slowly away from Hector's ring of protection. He would be there for some time, I later learned, working out a tenuous truce with the rival gang. He would do so without violence.

Twice more, when I was faced with a dangerous situation, Hector would appear as if out of thin air and in his unusual way protect my life. To this day I do not understand how he knew where I was or that I needed help.

Over the years I patrolled the neighborhood, I would sometimes run into Hector. More than once, I invited him and his wife to our home for dinner. Though Hector never felt comfortable enough to accept my invitation, I ate with his family regularly until I was transferred to another precinct.

Several years later, just before taking a government position overseas, I went back to the housing project to tell Hector goodbye. I walked the battered stairway to the familiar apartment but found it vacant. The landlord could only tell me that Hector and his family had packed up and left earlier that week, leaving no forwarding address.

I often think of Hector and wonder where he is today. I suspect that if I ever again find myself in a dangerous situation with no way of escape, he might just show up and bail me out.

"Are you my guardian angel or something?" I asked Hector one night, sitting on the fire escape behind his apartment.

"No," he said, looking at a distant star in the night sky. "I am Superman."

~Jamie Winship

The Kindness of Strangers

Joanne answered the door still clutching the letter in her hand. When she saw the grinning, rumpled young man standing at her door, a smile replaced the worried expression on her face.

Richard was a top photographer in New York City. His fashion and celebrity photographs had graced book covers and the pages of *Vogue, Harpers Bazaar, Vanity Fair,* and *Town and Country.* Though he was welcome in the homes of the rich and famous and had a studio on posh Fifth Avenue, he dressed the part of the starving artiste. On that freezing December day just weeks before Christmas, he wore jeans, a cotton shirt under a heavy fisherman's knit sweater, a light windbreaker, a knitted stocking cap, no gloves, and dirty white sneakers.

"Aren't you freezing?" Joanne asked as she led him inside.

"Nah," he said, brushing it off.

Later, over a steaming cup of cocoa, he asked, "Is something the matter? You don't seem yourself today."

"I'm fine. It's just that," she said, pointing to the letter lying on the coffee table. "I received it this morning, and I don't know what to do about it."

Richard picked up the letter, noticing the early November date on it. He read:

> *Urgent Appeal!!!*
>
> *A group of five high school students, followers of Dr. Martin Luther King, Jr., were arrested yesterday in McComb, Mississippi, during a peaceful demonstration against state segregation laws. The charges against them will not hold up in any court of law, but local authorities are determined to keep these young people jailed through Christmas.*
>
> *Bail has been set deliberately high with the knowledge that these youngsters and their families have no financial resources. In order to secure the release of these young people in time for them to spend Christmas with their families, we need to raise $14,000 bail and present it in cash or money order to the authorities by December 23.*
>
> *Time is short. Can you help?*

He read no further.

"Where did you get this?" he asked.

"A friend forwarded it to me, hoping I could do something," Joanne said. "These are just a bunch of idealistic teenagers. I hate to think of them in jail, especially on Christmas. But I just got the letter today, and I don't see how I could come up with that much money that quickly."

Richard thought carefully for a moment.

"Can I borrow the letter?" he asked. "I've got lots of clients with lots of money, and many of them do care."

"Of course, take it. But you'd have to mail it by the seventeenth for it to get to Mississippi by the twenty-third. That leaves only a week to raise the money. It's too late."

"Maybe, but it's worth a shot."

During the next few days the photographer ran about the city nonstop. He called on famous actors and actresses, society belles, magazine editors, best-selling writers, media barons, and captains of industry. Everywhere he went he took the crumpled letter out of his pocket and left with a sizable check in his hand.

In the late afternoon of Friday, December 17, he picked up the last donation. If he got the money order in the mail that day, the kids could be out by Christmas! He called the closest post office to find out when the money-order window closed. He had just enough time.

He dodged heavy traffic and darted through crowds of New Yorkers scurrying to buy last-minute holiday gifts. The snow began to fall, and the arctic wind swept away the traffic fumes, leaving the air unusually clean and fresh. Although the frigid cold cut straight through his windbreaker and sweater, perspiration trickled down his sides as he raced through the streets. As he dashed up the slippery steps of the post office, he glanced at his watch: just after 5:00. He had made it!

Glad to be out of the cold, he stamped the snow from his wet sneakers and scanned the cavernous room for the money-order window. His heart fell. It was barred and completely dark. He looked around for someone else to help him, but the adjacent windows were also closed and no one was at the main counter. He spotted a young man sorting mail far in the back, under a single hanging bulb.

"Hey!" the photographer called. "Where's the guy who handles money orders?"

"Gone home."

"But I called, and he said he'd be here for another half hour!"

"Yeah, man, but it started snowing, so he went home. Come again on Monday."

"Can you get him to come back today?"

"No way. He lives all the way out on Long Island."

"Can you help me with a money order?"

"Nope. I'm not authorized to do money orders. Don't even have the key to open the drawer."

The photographer stood helplessly in the empty room. If only he'd come a half-hour earlier. He'd failed. And now those five kids in Mississippi would spend their Christmas in a stark, lonely jail cell instead of at home with their families, where they belonged. Dejected, he turned to leave.

"Sorry. I'd help if I could," said the postal worker, who had moved to the front counter.

Richard turned around and looked intently at him.

"You okay, man?" the clerk asked.

"Yeah, I'm fine. But have you heard about the kids in McComb, Mississippi?"

After the photographer finished his story, the clerk reached for the telephone, told him to hold on a minute, and dialed a number.

"Hi, Marla. Can I speak with Pete?" he said. "Hey Pete! This is Joe. Hey, have you heard about the kids in McComb, Mississippi?"

When Joe hung up the phone, he pointed to the bench and said, "Have a seat. He's coming back."

It was a long wait. A blanket of snow was falling from a starless, black sky when Pete finally arrived.

The young activists in McComb, Mississippi, were out of jail in time to attend church on Christmas Eve. They didn't know how, or from where, or from whom the bail money had come. They didn't know that one man had brought together the compassionate hearts of many people. They thought it had come to them through some kind of miracle. Perhaps it had.

~Elaine Slater

I Heard the Bells of Heaven

My mom had a good life, all in all. I reminded myself of that when we resorted to putting her in a nursing home when she was eighty-three years old. Dementia had overtaken her, and she needed more medical care and daily help than we, as family members, could give her. During her stay at the nursing home, she had a number of falls, each one setting her back a little more. She was hospitalized three times for pneumonia, and each time we didn't think she was going to make it. Every time she approached death's door, she begged me to stay by her side. She was terrified of being alone when she died, and she wanted me to be with her when her time came.

When Mom was eighty-nine, we moved her to an extended-care facility approximately five minutes from our home. It made it easier for me to visit her often, although at that point, she hadn't recognized me for two years. I once asked her if she knew who I was.

"Well, you look familiar. Who are you?" she asked.

"I'm Karen."

"Oh, I have a daughter named Karen."

"That's right, Mom. I am your daughter Karen."

"That's nice," she said. "Who are you?"

About nine months after Mother moved to the extended-care facility, she became completely bedridden. I honestly believe, at that point, all she wanted was to die. She could no longer speak, and she refused to eat. When pneumonia set in, she was immediately hospitalized. I went to see her every day at every mealtime, trying to coax some nourishment into her. She rallied for a short time but relapsed and was sent back to the extended-care facility to die. The doctors, nurses, and hospice workers said there was nothing more they could do for her, except to make her comfortable in her last few days. And they did.

She soon slipped into a coma. For more than two weeks, she was given oxygen to help her breathe more easily as well as steady doses of morphine for pain, but no life-sustaining intravenous fluids. The nurses swabbed her dry mouth with glycerin sponges.

My mom had been a fairly heavy woman at approximately 160 pounds; now she was skeletal. It was so difficult to see her lying there motionless, so frail and skinny. I agonized over the slow, torturous slipping away of this once-vibrant woman—my children's grandma, the person who had raised me and loved me unconditionally. Why couldn't she just die peacefully? Why did she have to linger on like this? When would it end? I searched for answers and found none.

I was a wreck. I spent hours sitting by her side, stroking her head and face, telling her how much I loved her, not knowing whether she heard or felt the touch of the daughter she no longer knew. The last few days of her life were almost unbearable. I would no sooner get home for a break from my vigil than one of the nurses would call to tell me it was time and to come as quickly as possible.

One Friday afternoon I'd been home only fifteen minutes when they called to summon me back. The end was near. I drove like a maniac, barely able to see through the flood of tears rolling down my face. My mind raced: *Will I make it in time? I've got to make it in time. Hold on, Mom; please hold on till I get there. I won't leave you alone. I promised. I have to be there for you. I need to be there with you.*

When I arrived, I shuddered with a mixture of

relief and grief when I saw that Mom was still with us. A new nurse was looking after her; she was very kind and told me it would be any time now. The nurses had closed off her bed for privacy, as she was in a room with three other elderly ladies. The room was absolutely still; the only sound the hiss of the respirator helping my mother breathe. I thought I would go nuts. My husband, Ross, my rock, came right after work to be with me. I looked after Mom; he looked after me.

My brother, Jim, had said his goodbyes earlier in the week. (He wasn't much good at this kind of thing, but then again, who is?) My sons had come the day before to kiss their grandma goodbye; it was breaking their hearts, too. When the end came, it would be just Mom and me. I'd be with her, but she wouldn't even know it. Not only had she not known me for more than two years, but she hadn't responded to anyone or anything for two weeks. Overwhelmed by feelings of devastating loss, I wept uncontrollably. I needed my mom to know she was going to be okay, for her to know she wasn't alone.

Ross and I sat for hours, not speaking, watching and waiting, our silence punctuated only by my occasional bouts of crying. We were both tired, and neither of us had eaten. I told Ross, when he asked, that I had no stomach for food. At that point the nurse came in to give Mom some morphine and a warm sponge bath and to reposition her. She suggested we go out for some fresh air and something to eat, assuring us there was time. We were gone an hour.

When we returned, at 10:00 P.M., they had wheeled my mother's bed into the dining room so as not to disturb her roommates. Ross and I continued our silent deathbed watch into the night. At 2:00 A.M., I looked over at my exhausted husband, still in his suit and tie from work, and told him to go home to get some rest. He made me promise to call him if anything changed.

The nurses were so caring. They brought me a recliner from down the hall and covered me with a warm blanket. I settled back into the recliner and just lay there, watching her, waiting. I don't know when I dozed off, but I was awakened when the fire alarm went off so loudly I bolted straight up in the recliner. I glanced first at the clock: 4:30. *Oh no!* I thought. *Oh God, please don't let her have died while I was sleeping!*

I looked immediately toward my mother and couldn't believe what I saw, wondering if I could possibly be dreaming. I got up from the chair, never taking my eyes from my mother's face. Her eyes were open, and as I moved to her side, her eyes followed me.

"Oh Mom, you're awake, you're awake. I'm here, Mommy, I'm here with you, I won't leave you."

Her breathing was very shallow. She looked like a little guppy opening and closing her mouth, and I was concerned that she was struggling to breathe. I leaned closer and looked into her eyes, which were now moist and very alive.

"Mom, I'm going to get the nurse. We're going to make you more comfortable. I'll be right back, I promise. Hold on, I'll be right back."

I looked out the door, hoping to flag down a nurse, but there were none in sight. I hated to leave Mom for a single minute, but I was afraid she was in pain and struggling. I ran down the hall, looking for someone, anyone. I finally found my mother's nurse on her coffee break, talking with another nurse.

"Come quick, my mom is awake!"

"Awake? That's impossible. She's been in a coma for two weeks."

"Well, she's awake now, and she's having a hard time. When did you last give her a morphine shot?"

"I looked in on her an hour ago, and she didn't seem to need it."

"Well, she needs it now."

"I'll get it and be right down."

As I left the coffee room, I heard Mom's nurse say to the other nurse, "I don't believe this."

For some reason, I didn't rush back to the room; I walked casually down the long corridor. Maybe I had finally hit the wall and simply didn't have the energy. Maybe I was afraid she'd passed on while I was rounding up the nurse and couldn't face the guilt. But when I entered the room, I could see she had waited for me.

Her eyes followed me as I drew closer. She was barely breathing.

"It's okay, Mom. I'm here with you. I love you; I will always love you. We all love you very much."

I kissed her forehead and gently stroked her hair.

"Don't worry about anything. I'm OK; the whole family is OK. It's OK for you to go now."

With that, she took her last breath. I closed her eyelids, and a split second later her nurse arrived with the shot of morphine.

"She doesn't need it now. My mom is gone."

"I'm so sorry," the nurse said, patting my shoulder.

She checked my mother's pulse and listened to her heart. But it was all over. I knew it. I'd felt her leave. I stretched out on the bed beside my mom and held her till my husband arrived. Although I was grieving terribly, I felt an inner peace come over me, and I knew with certainty that my mother was finally at peace, too. Ross held me in his arms while I cried like a baby. When it was time to leave, I covered her sweet face with the blanket, and we walked to the nurses' station.

We stopped to fill out some forms and to thank the staff, who had cared so wonderfully for my mom. Just as we turned to leave, I remembered the fire alarm.

"Was there a fire, or was it just a false alarm?" I asked.

"I'm sorry, but I don't know what you're talking about," the nurse said.

"The fire alarm," I said matter-of-factly.

"No fire alarm went off here. Believe me, we would've heard it."

"You didn't hear a loud bell clanging?" I insisted. "It was so loud, it jolted me awake."

"Nope. No bells were ringing around here tonight," the nurse said. "When did you hear it?"

"Just before my mother died—just before I ran to get you when she woke up."

"Maybe your mom was trying to wake you up, so you could be with her when she passed on."

Ross and I looked at each other: of course. Mom had wanted to share her last moments with me. She had wanted to let me know she knew I was there. She had wanted to tell me that she was OK and that she loved me. She had wanted to say goodbye.

We will never know exactly what happened that night or why. All I know for sure is that in the final moments of her life, my mother looked at me with love and recognition in her eyes. And it gave me a sense of peace, gratitude, and hope that will stay with me for the rest of my life.

~Karen Thorstad

One Night Before Christmas

For the first time in my life I was going to spend Christmas alone—certainly not by choice and certainly not happily.

I was in my mid-twenties, and until then I'd spent every important holiday of every year in the close company of family and friends. I always had grand plans for Christmas, and that year I had intended to take a special getaway with a special friend. On the afternoon of Christmas Eve, my friend called with bad news: there was a serious illness in his family, and he had to fly home immediately. Because the airlines were impossibly booked up, he'd been lucky to get a flight with several connections. He said he felt horrible about racing off at the last minute.

I understood; how could I not? I wished him Godspeed and that his Christmas would be made merrier by his loved one's speedy recovery. But I felt horrible, too, and very, very alone.

The more I thought about it, the more sullen I became. Christmas is a time for getting together with loved ones. What was there to celebrate alone? What was I going to do? Where was I going to go? Who would I share Christmas Eve cocoa and cookies with? Who would I share Christmas gifts and dinner and laughter and hugs with? What was Christmas alone? It wasn't Christmas at all!

It was too late to check with other friends to see whether they could squeeze one more into their happy gatherings. Well, I could have asked; I'm sure any one of them would have welcomed me into their holiday festivities, but I didn't feel comfortable calling at the eleventh hour. I didn't want to impose. I didn't want to look that needy. I didn't want to feel like the outsider observing another family's holiday traditions. I wanted to observe my own Christmas traditions with the people closest to my heart.

I was an only child, and the other members of my small family now lived many miles away. At that point, there was no way I could go to them or they could come to me for Christmas. I was alone.

There was nothing to do but get through it. Trying to cheer myself up, I plugged in the lights on my tiny Christmas tree and switched on the string of lights framing the front window of my small apartment. I turned on the radio to a station playing Christmas music and heated a mug of mulled cider. As I sat at the kitchen table, sipping the hot, spicy cider, I recalled the joyful Christmases of my childhood.

The season always began with the quest for the perfect Christmas tree. Tradition dictated that Dad and I complete this mission while Mom stayed behind to "take care of some things." It was many years before I realized that she used this time to wrap the presents she had already bought for me. I didn't mind tramping through the woods in drizzling rain or sloshing through mud in search of the ultimate tree. I was thrilled to have my dad all to myself. With his goofiness and funny stories, Dad was a riot to be with, and I laughed so much I hardly noticed the wet and cold. After a considerable amount of clowning and searching, we always found The One: tall, perfectly symmetrical, and full of bushy needles.

When my parents and I decorated the tree together, we would share the memories we associated with various ornaments. In top comedic form, Dad provided us with lots of laughter as we worked, and Mother would take a break from the tree trimming to serenade us with Christmas carols on the piano. We would end the evening by sipping hot cocoa topped with marshmallows as we gazed at our handiwork.

Another father-daughter tradition was the annual shopping excursion. On a carefully chosen day, Dad and I would go downtown to shop for our gifts for Mom. This called for careful attention to detail, because although my mother always gave us ideas about what she wanted, my father still needed my assistance in making his selections. I had far less trouble choosing my gift for Mom. For several years I insisted on buying a brand of hand lotion she liked, not considering that she already had quite a collection of it from my past presentations on Mother's Day, Easter, and her birthday. When dad was finally able to change my mind about the lotion, I switched to her favorite perfume, eventually managing to give her a lifetime supply of that as well. The shopping trip usually ended with my father buying me a small toy or treat.

Mom and I had our shopping trip, too, but it didn't seem quite as special because I went to stores with her all the time. Besides, she didn't buy me ice cream or a yo-yo.

Baking Christmas cookies with my mother was a treat, though, because I normally didn't get to help her in the kitchen. We would talk and laugh as we conjured up tasty goodies such as buttery shortbread, sweet coconut rolls, and almond cookies, the savory fragrances swirling around us. When the last tray of cookies went into the oven, I would sit cross-legged on the kitchen floor with the giant mixing bowl in my lap, sweeping my finger around the sides to gather the last of the delicious batter.

Christmas Day was a flurry of festivity. It began at the crack of dawn, with a thrilling blur of gifts from Santa, colorful wrapping paper, fuzzy stockings brimming with tiny treasures, and miniature Christmas oranges everywhere—all punctuated by the ever-present scent of fresh pine. After church services, we would go to my grandparents' home for a turkey dinner followed by the exchange of more presents. Late in the afternoon we would head out of town to my other grandfather's place for another turkey dinner and gift exchange. On the drive home that night I would nod sleepily in the back seat of the car, stuffed with turkey and joy.

Those memories of warm Christmases past only served to sink my spirits as I sat alone in my kitchen that Christmas Eve. I put my head down in my arms on the table and sobbed.

After a while, when I was all cried out, I lifted my head and looked out the window. I saw that the navy-blue sky was filled with sparkling stars, and smiled when I spotted one that shone considerably brighter than the others. The sight of the soft, fresh snow piled high like cotton on the ground and covering the evergreen boughs like fine lace was a cool balm to my sore eyes. I noticed how the lights twinkled on my neighbors' houses, and how their Christmas trees were framed in their windows like charming postcards— and I realized that my outlook was brightening.

Christmas had come to me after all. In that moment I began to comprehend that Christmas wasn't about celebrating with gifts or even with people: it was about celebrating love. And love I had plenty of, whether or not any of my loved ones were with me at the moment to share it with.

Wrapped in a comforting blanket of peace and, yes, even joy, I curled up on the couch in the company of my perfect little Christmas tree.

My reverie was disturbed by the ringing of the phone. I jumped with surprise, because everyone knew I had planned to be away on Christmas Eve. It was my mom, cheerfully saying she felt she should phone even though she knew of my plans for the evening. As we chatted, I felt the warm connection that contact with close family brings.

Just as I settled back on the couch again, there was another phone call. Assuming that my mother had forgotten to tell me something, I was surprised to hear a friend's voice. He explained that he'd been enjoying the evening with his family when he felt the urge to call, even though he knew I'd planned to be away that night. We hadn't spoken for over a week, so we caught up on each other's news and wished one another a happy holiday.

By the time the third call came, I was wondering whether a little birdie had peeked in my kitchen window while I was in such despair and put out an SOS to my loved ones. Again, the caller mentioned that she'd gotten a strong feeling that she should phone right away. The fourth person to call had actually left the table in the middle of a meal because the impulse to call was so strong, while the fifth had been driving home when she suddenly felt the need to pull over and call me from a pay phone.

By the time I finally went to bed that Christmas Eve, fourteen people—some of whom I hadn't seen for a year or more—had phoned. All had volunteered the information that they'd experienced a sudden, strong desire to call right away, but none had sensed that I was in peril or distress. They had simply felt the urgent need to reach out and connect with me.

Since then, I have spent a number of Christmases by myself and have been perfectly content to do so. The warm memory of the love I felt that Christmas Eve so many years ago has kept me from ever feeling alone again.

~Judi Chapman

Ah, the Dandy Lions!

I long ago stopped thinking of dandelions as my enemies. While lawn perfectionists see them only as challenging pests, to me they represent innocence and beauty and wonder. The sight, or even the mere thought, of dandelions brings back to me poignant memories of a time when a child's faith, bolstered by a grownup's guidance, made the impossible seem possible and magical.

Ah, the "dandy lions" as my young daughter used to call them.

"Mom, what's a dandy?" she would ask.

I would dutifully explain that a dandy was a very fancy English gentleman from a long time ago. He was the kind of man who wore a colorful scarf, called an ascot, around his neck, a shiny tall hat, called a top hat, and fine gloves to keep his manicured hands smooth and soft. A dandy always covered his shoes with white leather wraps, called spats, to protect them from dirt and scuffs. To finish off his outfit, he always looped a fresh flower of the season into a buttonhole on his jacket.

Inevitably, she would draw her two little hands from behind her back and present me with a crumpled fistful of the brightest yellow dandelions.

"For you, Mom," she'd say, "A whole bouquet of brand-new flowers for your buttonholes."

I never had the heart to tell her that no upstanding dandy would ever have been caught with one of these weeds on his person.

Instead, I would embrace her along with the bright little flowers on their squashed stems. At least once every summer throughout my daughter's childhood, this little play would be acted out.

My daughter never asked about the lion part of the name or what it might have to do with a dandy, so I never felt compelled to explain. She didn't realize her spelling error until about the fourth grade when she learned the textbook definition of the word. The two of us knew that *dandy lion* was the correct interpretation, and that d-a-n-d-e-l-i-o-n was probably just a harder way of spelling it. I told her, however, that in the meantime she would have to spell it the teacher's way when she was in school.

She, like all little people, looked forward to the

end of summer when the dandy lions turned to seed. When she was very young, I had told her that the white puffy ball that replaced the yellow flower held magic and would bring her wonderful gifts.

"Hold the dandy like this," I'd instructed, placing the spent flower near my face. "Then make a secret wish, take a deep breath, and blow. When all the white pieces of the flower take to the air and fly up to Heaven, God will grant your special wish."

Every summer, I watched her repeat this ritual, usually with some awkwardness but always with great seriousness. She somehow understood at a very young age that God wouldn't always deliver her wish exactly the way she'd requested it, but that what she'd eventually receive would be close enough. In hindsight, I believe that her faith in her dandy-lion wishes laid the foundation for the growth of her spiritual faith.

One lazy August day in the year my daughter turned seven, I watched her meander about in our backyard field, where the bright yellow dandies had already turned to seed. She traveled carefully so as not to disturb any of the tiny "angel wings," as she called them. She surveyed the field carefully, looking for just the right dandy. A few times, she picked one too hard, sending its angel wings flying on the wind before she could make a wish.

I saw her carefully pluck one with a full white puffball atop a firm, bright-green stem. She carefully positioned herself as if in a thoughtful yoga pose and closed her eyes as if to concentrate on the best wish ever, all the while holding tightly to her flower. Unfortunately, she held the weed a bit too close to her nose, and when she opened her eyes to make her wish come true, her breath had already sent half the angel wings into the air. The look of exasperation on her face told me that the task was perhaps bigger than she could handle.

I waited some time for her to share her thoughts, to ask for help, but she apparently needed to work it out herself. No little dandy lion was going to outsmart her and keep her from her perfect wish! I watched a while longer as she stubbornly attempted to conquer the dandy lion patch, one by one, to no avail.

Knowing that the dandy lion season was nearing its end, I finally asked her if she'd made at least one wish. She shook her head no.

"This year I'm doing something different, Mom," she solemnly said.

"Oh . . . what's that?" I asked her.

She explained that unless she could wish upon one complete, perfectly rounded dandy lion without a single angel wing missing, it wouldn't work.

"What won't work, sweetie?" I asked her.

"This year, I want *all* my wishes to come true *forever*! I know if I blow on the perfect one, that will happen!"

I gave her a hug. For a brief moment, my eyes filled with tears and my heart ached as I thought, *Oh, if only that were true; if only it were that easy*. The sweet sound of her voice suddenly pulled me from my sad reverie.

"What are we gonna do, Mom? How am I gonna do it?"

While we snuggled a minute or two longer, an idea came to me.

"Maybe we need to catch him by surprise," I told her. "Maybe, just maybe, he doesn't want us to pick him."

"But if I can't pick him up, how can I blow my wishes to Heaven?"

"How about we stand here very still while you pick out the one you think might be the best. Then we'll creep along the ground together and sneak up on that sly old dandy."

"Then what, Mom? What good will that do us? He still won't let us pick him."

"Well, we won't pick him," I said. "We'll make our wishes before we crawl over to him. Then, when we get close, we'll hold our breath, and when we're right next to him, you can lean down and let all your breath go. That way, you'll catch him by surprise!"

A joyful look crossed her face. She took a mere minute to select her favorite dandy, then we rechecked the game plan with each other to make sure our espionage was foolproof.

Slowly we began our creep, initially on our hands and knees, but as we drew closer, we moved on our bellies. When we were within a foot of our destination, I gave the signal that it was time to hold our breath by pinching my nose. My daughter did the same. With tender amusement, I watched her face flush and blow up like a bright-pink balloon. As she slid closer to her target, her puffed-out cheeks turned bluish-white and looked like they might explode, but the serious look in her eyes and her deliberate forward movement made it clear that she was determined to achieve her goal. About six inches from our final destination, I gave her the nod. In the flick of a millisecond, she released all the air her cheeks had been able to hold.

Her eyes danced with glee as 10,000 angel wings seemed to take flight—not just from the perfect dandy lion she'd selected, but also from the twenty or thirty dandies surrounding it.

"Quickly, flip over," I said.

Then, lying on our backs and holding hands, we watched as all her wishes floated straight into the sky and up to heaven. I gazed at her innocent face and said a silent prayer: *Dear God, if you believe in little girls, especially ones who make wishes, please bless this one lying among the remnants of the dandy lions.*

We had found the perfect dandy lion just in time. That evening there was a downpour, and the next day all that remained of the dandy lions were hundreds of topless green stems.

This year, if all the perfect-lawn people bent on whacking, uprooting, and poisoning dandelions could leave a few for me, I would really appreciate it. You see, my little girl is all grown up now, and the only dandelion bouquets I get are the ones I pick every summer for myself. I wouldn't miss a year without them, because every time I see those angel wings take flight, I know that somewhere some seven-year-old's wishes are coming true.

~Laureeann Porter

Tell Your Story in the Next
Cup of Comfort®

We hope you have enjoyed *A Cup of Comfort*®: *Classic Edition* and that you will share it with all the special people in your life.

You won't want to miss our next heartwarming volumes, *A Cup of Comfort*® *for Single Mothers*, *A Cup of Comfort*® *for Horse Lovers*, and *A Cup of Comfort*® *for Cat Lovers*. Look for these new books in your favorite bookstores soon!

We're brewing up lots of other *Cup of Comfort*® books, each filled to the brim with true stories that will touch your heart and soothe your soul. The inspiring tales included in these collections are written by everyday men and women, and we would love to include one of your stories in an upcoming edition of *A Cup of Comfort*®.

Do you have a powerful story about an experience that dramatically changed or enhanced your life? A compelling story that can stir our emotions, make us think, and bring us hope? An inspiring story that reveals lessons of humility within a vividly told tale? Tell us your story!

Each *Cup of Comfort*® contributor will receive a monetary fee, author credit, and a complimentary copy of the book. Just e-mail your submission of 1,000 to 2,000 words (one story per e-mail; no attachments, please) to *cupofcomfort@adamsmedia. com*. Or, if e-mail is unavailable to you, send it to:

A Cup of Comfort
Adams Media
57 Littlefield Street
Avon, MA 02322

You can submit as many stories as you'd like, for whichever volumes you'd like. Make sure to include your name, address, and other contact information and indicate for which volume you'd like to be considered. We also welcome your suggestions for new *Cup of Comfort*® themes.

For more information, please visit our Web site: *www.cupofcomfort.com*.

We look forward to sharing many more soothing *Cups of Comfort*® with you!

Contributors

Stephanie Barrow ("An Angel's Voice") could never decide which of her two passions to focus on—writing or painting—so she pursued both. She currently works as an illustrator and sometime feature writer for the *Register-Guard* newspaper in Eugene, Oregon, were she lives near her children and two grandchildren.

Teri Bayus ("Miracle Fish") lives in Pismo Beach, California. She has owned a public relations firm for more than a decade and writes a humor/travel column for *What's On* magazine. She produces *Silver Treasures*, a television show featuring people over the age of eighty telling their amazing life stories, and she is currently working on a screenplay about the woes of teenage life.

Renie Szilak Burghardt ("A Special Present") was born in Hungary and immigrated to the United States in 1951. She lives in the country, where she enjoys nature, reading, and family activities. Her writing has been published in numerous magazines and anthologies, including *Whispers from Heaven* and *Listening to the Animals*.

Barbara W. Campbell ("The Light of Innocence") was born and raised in the southern United States. She and her husband John moved with their six children to Australia in 1975. When the grandchildren started arriving, Barbara began storytelling. Now with eleven grandchildren and most of the family living in and around Brisbane, she finds time to put the stories to paper.

Christy Caballero ("A Love That Burns Eternal") is a freelance writer who lives a few deer trails off the beaten path in rural Oregon. She has received state and national journalism awards through the National Federation of Press Women.

Judi Chapman ("The Sweet Pea" and "One Night Before Christmas") is a freelance writer of both fiction and nonfiction. Her short stories, which have been published nationwide, celebrate the joys and mysteries of life. She hails from Edmonton, Alberta, Canada.

Mary Jane Chew ("The Well Driller") graduated from Purdue University with a bachelor of science degree in marketing and journalism. She lives in Asheville, North Carolina, where she writes part-time for the marketing industry. She spends the other part of her time admiring the Blue Ridge Mountains and writing about life.

Bobbie Christmas ("The Greatest Christmas Gift") is a book editor and coauthor of *The Legend of Codfish and Potatoes*. She is the current president of the Georgia Writers Association and owner of Zebra Communications, a literary services company.

Susan A. Duncan ("An Angel's Kiss") is the author of *Levittown: The Way We Were*, as well as several nonfiction stories. She lives with her family in New York.

Susan Farr-Fahncke ("Make a Wish, Mommy") is a writer, wife, and mother of four living in Utah. Her inspirational stories have appeared in many books and magazines. She is currently working on a book-length collection of her stories.

Rusty Fischer ("A Heaping Helping of Thanksgiving" and "Gratitude Harvest") is the author of more than 100 published articles, essays, stories, and poems, which have appeared in anthologies, national magazines, and online publications. He is the author of *Creative Writing Made Easy*, the best-selling series for students and teachers of writing, as well as four Buzz On reference guides. Rusty has also written for several Internet portals.

Lynda Kudelko Foley ("In the Arms of Grace") lives in Northridge, California, with her husband and two sons. The 1994 Northridge earthquake motivated Lynda to seriously pursue writing. Shortly thereafter, she won a screenwriting internship at Paramount Studios. Her short fiction has been included in anthologies by Pocket Books and Aunt Lute Books.

Margaret A. Frey ("Holding Your Breath") writes from the foothills of the Smokey Mountains. Her fiction and nonfiction work has appeared in numerous print and online publications, including *Notre Dame Magazine*, *Thema*, *Mindprints*, *Cezanne's Carrot*, and *Raving Dove*. She lives with her husband, John, and canine literary critic, Ruffian.

Jenna Glatzer ("Finding Our Home") is a full-time freelance writer, the editor-in-chief of AbsoluteWrite.com, and the public relations director for the film *Curse of the Dog Women*. Her work has appeared in hundreds of magazines and Web sites, including Salon.com, *Writer's Digest*, and *American Profile*.

Theresa Marie Heim ("Memoir of a Violin") is a graduate student living in Santa Monica, California. A freelance writer, she contributes articles and essays to online and print publications.

Lynn M. Huffstetler ("My Dad, the Pink Lady") is an award-winning author of outdoor hunting stories, inspirational and nostalgic tales, and science-fiction stories and novels. He lives in the east Tennessee mountains.

David Kirkland ("A Daughter's Trust") is a former schoolteacher, welfare worker, banker, and real-estate developer who has lived in Guam, New York, Hawaii, and North Carolina. He currently resides in Missouri, where he is at work on a Civil War novel set in East Tennessee.

M. A. Kosak ("The Colors of Prejudice") teaches creative writing to elementary school children in after-school enrichment programs. As a freelance writer, she centers her work on personal experience, particularly adoption, infertility, education, and personal relationships. Originally from New Jersey, she resides in San Diego, California, with her husband and three adopted sons.

Susanmarie Lamagna ("Listen to Your Heart") is a bilingual Spanish kindergarten teacher in the San Francisco Bay Area. Growing up in a busy but loving family, she learned the value of sharing not only one's things but also one's self, a lesson she is passing along to her students—who, she says, also teach her.

Helene LeBlanc ("The White Dress") is a two-time winner of the Jessamyn West fiction award and the author of

Summer Boy and *From the Grape to the Glass*. Helene lives on a vineyard in Napa Valley, California, where she is currently writing a biographical novel about her family's experiences during the Depression.

Ella Magee ("Maddie's Rose") is the pseudonym of a writer and college instructor.

Joy Hewitt Mann ("Hidden Treasure") grew up near Georgian Bay, where her story takes place. She shares a mill house surrounded by nature's treasures with her husband, Wayne, and their three children. She has published two books of poetry and one fiction collection, and she has contributed to more than 200 magazines internationally.

Dolores Martin ("A Voice in the Storm"), a native of Illinois, lives with her daughter in Colorado Springs, where she works as a freelance writer. She recently completed her first children's book, *The Land That Might Have Been*. She has three children and two grandchildren.

Louise Mathewson ("Monsters of the Sky") holds a master's degree in pastoral studies from Loyola University and writes about the sacred moments found in the ordinary experiences of daily life. She and her husband have two adult children and live in Longmont, Colorado.

Anthony Merlocco ("A Special Day") lives in a small, rural community east of Toronto with Yvette, his wife of thirty-five years. They have two adult children. Anthony enjoys writing, composing music, playing piano, fishing, and country life.

Lynn Ruth Miller ("Sing Your Song") is an award-winning fiction writer, journalist, essayist, and columnist. She has worked in public relations and served as the promotions director of the San Francisco International Film Festival. Her column "Thoughts While Walking the Dog" appears regularly in the *Pacifica Tribune*. She teaches adults in San Mateo County, California.

Toña Morales-Calkins ("Guiding Lights") is a freelance writer living in Northern California. When not writing, Toña works as a bookstore manager and trainer. "Guiding Lights" is her first published story. She is currently working on two novels.

Ed Nickum ("Quiet Courage") is the author of dozens of short stories and is currently working on a horror novel. He makes his home in Cincinnati, Ohio, with his wife and two daughters.

Mary Marcia Lee Norwood ("The Crying Chair") is a wife, mother, grandmother, and professional storyteller. Her work as a writer and photojournalist has been featured in newspapers and international magazines, including *Chosen Child, Adoption Today*, the *Red Thread*, the *Kansas City Star*, the *Examiner*, and *Mother & Child Reunion*. A former teacher and coach, Marcia served as the regional coordinator for the educational outreach program of the National Inventors Hall of Fame.

Janet Oakley ("Drywall in the Time of Grief") lives in Bellingham, Washington. She found her life again in writing historical fiction and helping high school students decipher nineteenth-century court cases for a History Channel grant. She enjoys gardening and is currently putting in drywall in a mysterious section of her turn-of-the-century house.

Laureeann Porter ("Ah, the Dandy Lions!") is internationally recognized in the hospice-care field as a founder of hospice. She has a passion for nostalgic storytelling, and her writing has been published in regional magazines. She often makes appearances as an oral storyteller in regional bookstores and libraries. Originally a Bostonian, she now lives in Florida.

Norman Prady ("Grandpa's Suitcase") first began to write at the age of nine when his father brought home a second-hand Underwood typewriter. He's had successful careers as both a newspaper reporter and an advertising executive, sidelining as a freelance journalist and essayist. He recently completed a collection of autobiographical essays and sketches as well as a children's alphabet book.

Kathryn Thompson Presley ("A Softer Heart"), a retired English professor, has published numerous short stories, essays, and poems. She enjoys reading, speaking to women's groups, and playing Scrabble with her grandchildren. She has been married for almost fifty years to Roy Presley, a retired school superintendent.

LeAnn R. Ralph ("The Walk of Courage") is a staff writer for two weekly newspapers who also writes freelance stories about what it would have been like to grow up on the dairy farm homesteaded by her Norwegian great-grandparents in the late 1800s. She resides in Wisconsin, the state of her birth and childhood.

Kimberly Ripley ("A Gift from Christmas Angels") is the author of *Breathe Deeply, This Too Shall Pass*, a collection of tales on the trials and triumphs of parenting teenagers. She lives with her husband and their five children in Portsmouth, New Hampshire.

Edie Scher ("The Lady in the Blue Dress") became a collector of tales after listening to stories told at the kitchen table as a child. She loved retelling these stories and soon began writing them down. Her essays and articles have been published in several national magazines and newspapers, including Rodale and Hearst publications and the *New York Times*.

Bluma Schwarz ("Rejoice the Ides of March") is a semi-retired mental-health counselor who published her first memoir at the age of sixty-nine in *Iowa Woman*. Her stories have appeared in *Potpourri*, *Potomac Review*, *AIM*, and elsewhere. She continues to write and to counsel the mentally ill on a part-time basis in Florida, where she has made her home since 1964.

Elaine Slater's ("The Kindness of Strangers") wide and varied writing career began with short mystery stories and branched out into poetry, drama, short fiction, and how-to books. Her work has won several awards and has been widely anthologized. She resides in Toronto, Ontario, Canada.

Mary Helen Straker ("Home Place") is a graduate of DePauw University and a former newspaper and magazine writer. She has completed a novel and is currently writing a memoir. She and her husband live with their four children in Zanesville, Ohio.

Karen Thorstad ("I Heard the Bells of Heaven") is a licensed interior designer and cofounder of an Internet business who collects and writes stories about spiritual, paranormal, and transformational experiences. She lives with her husband, Ross, and their springer spaniel, Clyde, in British Columbia, Canada. They have six children and eight grandchildren.

Diane M. Vogel ("The Blue Washcloth") lives on the farm she shared with her late husband in rural mid-Michigan. In addition to running the farm, raising goats, and serving as a 4-H volunteer, she manages an Internet business, attends community college, and writes. The mother of three grown children, Diane recently remarried.

Denise Wahl ("A Stranger in the House," "More Precious Than Gold," and "Red Two-Seater") is a freelance writer and humor columnist. She lives in Michigan with her husband and four children.

Bob Welch ("Of Needs and Wants") is a columnist with the *Register-Guard* newspaper in Eugene, Oregon. He is the author of five books, including the Gold Medallion–winning *Father for All Seasons*.

Jamie Winship ("The Saint of Subsidized Housing") worked as a police officer for five years before leaving to earn a master's degree in English as a Second Language. He currently works at the Bandung Alliance International School in West Java, Indonesia.

Audrey Yanes ("The Windfall"), a child of the Depression she writes about in her story, went on to college and became a kindergarten teacher. Her own large family provides her with the interesting material and inspiration for her stories. Retired, she lives where she can see the Pacific Ocean from her upstairs window as she writes.

Lou Killian Zywicki ("Not Alone") is a freelance writer who also teaches writing, literature, and interpersonal communications at the Secondary Technical Center in Duluth, Minnesota. She lives in a nature paradise south of Carlton, Minnesota, with her husband, Ernie. She is the mother of four children.

About the Editor

Colleen Sell has compiled nineteen volumes of the *Cup of Comfort*® book series. She has also authored, ghostwritten, or edited more than 100 other books, published dozens of magazine articles, and served as editor-in-chief of two award-winning magazines. She lives with her husband, T. N. Trudeau, in a turn-of-the-century farmhouse on a 40-acre Oregon historic pioneer homestead, which they are slowly turning into an organic lavender and blueberry farm. Their border collie/Australian shepherd, Woodstock, watches over it all with amusement.

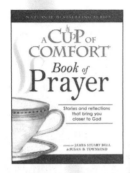

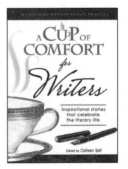